# CLIMBER'S GUIDE TO
# AMERICAN FORK CANYON
# ROCK CANYON

Mike Beck crimping hard on **Reanimator (5.12d) Hell Cave**

# CLIMBER'S GUIDE TO
# AMERICAN FORK CANYON
# ROCK CANYON

## STUART RUCKMAN
## BRET RUCKMAN

**FALCON**GUIDES ®

GUILFORD, CONNECTICUT
HELENA, MONTANA
AN IMPRINT OF THE GLOBE PEQUOT PRESS

FALCONGUIDES®


Previously published by Chockstone Press



FalconGuides is an imprint of The Globe Pequot Press
Falcon, FalconGuides, and Chockstone are registered trademarks of Morris Book Publishing, LLC

Front cover photograph of Merrill Bitter leading **Blue Typhoon [5.13a]** at **The Hideaway,** American Fork, Utah, and back cover photograph of Boone Speed leading **Monkey Brains [5.13a]** at **The Billboard,** American Fork Canyon, Utah, by Jeff Baldwin. Uncredited photos taken by the authors.

Library of Congress Catalog-in-Publication Data is available on file.

ISBN 978-0-934641-88-3

Printed in the United States of America

10 9 8 7 6 5 4

To our Mom, Ivy Ruckman,
whose creative energy is infectious.

# ACKNOWLEDGMENTS

THE PAINSTAKING COMPILATION of a guidebook requires as much time on the phone as it does on the rock. We owe many thanks to the following individuals who freely offered encouragement and enlightenment: David Bell, Merrill Bitter, Joe Brooks, Maria Cranor, Gordon Douglass, James Garrett, Douglas Hansen, James Kay, Scott Markewitz, Kim Miller, Scott Unice, and Geoff Weigand.

We give special thanks to Drew Bedford, Bill Boyle, Carl Horton, Darren Knezek, Bill Ohran, and Phil Reynolds whose previous guidebooks and articles formed the groundwork for this guide.

The indefatigable people's list: Jeff Baldwin, Bill Boyle, Doug Heinrich, Matt Neilson, Jeff Pedersen, Brian Smoot, and Boone Speed. These were the people we turned to constantly, and their patience in the face of our unending questions was remarkable.

We'd especially like to recognize the following people who went out of their way to provide us with information and encouragement: Jeff Baldwin, who patiently helped us through the intricate routes at the Hideaway; Darren Knezek, who provided us with a very complete list of new routes; Scott Lunt, who found our entire file of American Fork topos lying abandoned at the roadside; Matt Neilson, who Fed Exed a packet of information to us; Jeff Pedersen, who made sense of The Projects; and Mindy Shulak, who provided us with a detailed list, complete with comments, of all the new routes in American Fork Canyon.

To all these people we tip our hats and offer our most sincere thanks. Without their help, this guidebook never would have survived past the initial stages.

Finally, we'd like to thank our rock solid foundations--our families. The support of Kim Ruckman, Fred Thalmann, Ivy Ruckman, Judy Ruckman, and Libby Ellis, kept us motivated and focused. Without the acute editing skills of our mother and her forbearance when we turned her house into a "guidebook disaster zone," this book would have been a series of mixed metaphors, dangling participles and run-on sentences.

THANK YOU ALL!

In memory of Steve Carruthers

# WARNING: CLIMBING IS A SPORT WHERE YOU MAY BE SERIOUSLY INJURED OR DIE. READ THIS BEFORE YOU USE THIS BOOK.

This guidebook is a compilation of unverified information gathered from many different climbers. The author cannot assure the accuracy of any of the information in this book, including the topos and route descriptions, the difficulty ratings, and the protection ratings. These may be incorrect or misleading and it is impossible for any one author to climb all the routes to confirm the information about each route. Also, ratings of climbing difficulty and danger are always subjective and depend on the physical characteristics (for example, height), experience, technical ability, confidence and physical fitness of the climber who supplied the rating. Additionally, climbers who achieve first ascents sometimes underrate the difficulty or danger of the climbing route out of fear of being ridiculed if a climb is later down-rated by subsequent ascents. Therefore, be warned that you must exercise your own judgment on where a climbing route goes, its difficulty and your ability to safely protect yourself from the risks of rock climbing. Examples of some of these risks are: falling due to technical difficulty or due to natural hazards such as holds breaking, falling rock, climbing equipment dropped by other climbers, hazards of weather and lightning, your own equipment failure, and failure or absence of fixed protection.

**You should not depend on any information gleaned from this book for your personal safety; your safety depends on your own good judgment, based on experience and a realistic assessment of your climbing ability. If you have any doubt as to your ability to safely climb a route described in this book, do not attempt it.**

The following are some ways to make your use of this book safer:

1. **CONSULTATION:** You should consult with other climbers about the difficulty and danger of a particular climb prior to attempting it. Most local climbers are glad to give advice on routes in their area and we suggest that you contact locals to confirm ratings and safety of particular routes and to obtain first-hand information about a route chosen from this book.

2. **INSTRUCTION:** Most climbing areas have local climbing instructors and guides available. We recommend that you engage an instructor or guide to learn safety techniques and to become familiar with the routes and hazards of the areas described in this book. Even after you are proficient in climbing safely, occasional use of a guide is a safe way to raise your climbing standard and learn advanced techniques.

3. **FIXED PROTECTION:** Many of the routes in this book use bolts and pitons which are permanently placed in the rock. Because of variances in the manner of placement, weathering, metal fatigue, the quality of the metal used, and many other factors, these fixed protection pieces should always be considered suspect and should always be backed up by equipment that you place yourself. Never depend for your safety on a single piece of fixed protection because you never can tell whether it will hold weight, and in some cases, fixed protection may have been removed or is now absent.

Be aware of the following specific potential hazards which could arise in using this book:

1. **MISDESCRIPTIONS OF ROUTES:** If you climb a route and you have a doubt as to where the route may go, you should not go on unless you are sure that you can go that way safely. Route descriptions and topos in this book may be inaccurate or misleading.

2. **INCORRECT DIFFICULTY RATING:** A route may, in fact, be more difficult than the rating indicates. Do not be lulled into a false sense of security by the difficulty rating.

3. **INCORRECT PROTECTION RATING:** If you climb a route and you are unable to arrange adequate protection from the risk of falling through the use of fixed pitons or bolts and by placing your own protection devices, do not assume that there is adequate protection available higher just because the route protection rating indicates the route is not an "X" or an "R" rating. Every route is potentially an "X" (a fall may be deadly), due to the inherent hazards of climbing – including, for example, failure or absence of fixed protection, your own equipment's failure, or improper use of climbing equipment.

**THERE ARE NO WARRANTIES, WHETHER EXPRESS OR IMPLIED, THAT THIS GUIDEBOOK IS ACCURATE OR THAT THE INFORMATION CONTAINED IN IT IS RELIABLE. THERE ARE NO WARRANTIES OF FITNESS FOR A PARTICULAR PURPOSE OR THAT THIS GUIDE IS MERCHANTABLE. YOUR USE OF THIS BOOK INDICATES YOUR ASSUMPTION OF THE RISK THAT IT MAY CONTAIN ERRORS AND IS AN ACKNOWLEDGMENT OF YOUR OWN SOLE RESPONSIBILITY FOR YOUR CLIMBING SAFETY.**

Bill Boyle leading towards fame on **Sister Ray [5.12a] Red Corners Area**

Photo: Jeff Baldwin

# CONTENTS

# AREA OVERVIEW MAP

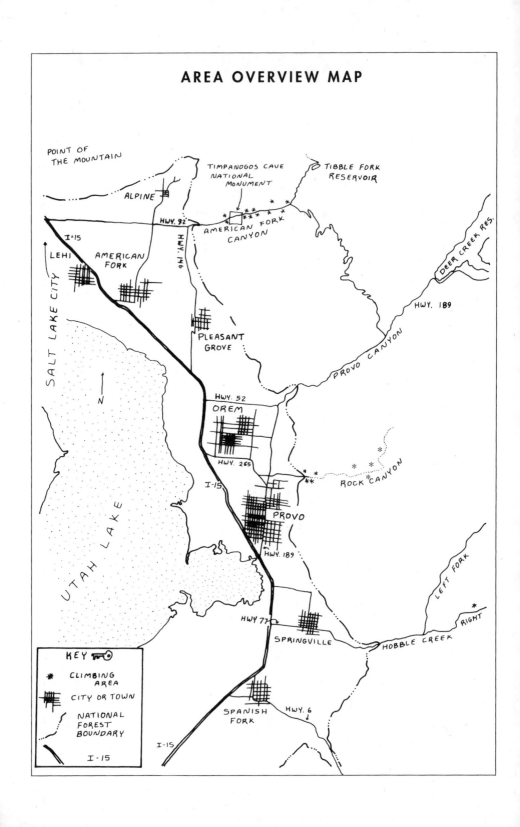

# INTRODUCTION

IN 1988 WHEN WE COMMITTED TO WRITING a rock climbing guidebook to the Wasatch Mountains, climbing in American Fork Canyon was nonexistent and Rock Canyon was home to 65 traditional routes on quartzite. As our work progressed on the granite areas around Salt Lake, we began to hear rumors of sport climbing in American Fork Canyon. Soon our friends were raving to us about the new limestone. We decided to add an additional chapter to our guidebook. By the Fall of 1990 when we presented George Meyers, our editor, with a stack of guidebook information, he looked at us and said, "Boys, there's enough here for two guides." Wasatch Climbing South was born. The next spring when the guidebook was published, 192 routes had been established in American Fork Canyon and the area was being visited regularly by the country's best climbers. The French superstars had left their mark and both *Climbing* and *Rock and Ice* magazines had printed articles about Utah's limestone. Excitement was high.

Now, in the fall of 1994, media attention has focused elsewhere and locals have a hard time remembering when they weren't climbing pockets in some dark cave. In the space of four years American Fork Canyon has seen a doubling of routes. Rock Canyon boasts 115 new lines on the limestone. With no end in sight to the amount of available rock, climbing in Utah Valley won't stagnate anytime soon.

During our tenure as guidebook authors, we have seen the southern half of the Wasatch Mountains transformed from a limited climbing area to a major climbing destination. Excitement, and quality, remain high.

## THE NATURE OF THE AREA

The Wasatch Mountains run south from roughly the Utah/Idaho border to south of Nephi, Utah. They are the pride and joy of many Utahns and provide easily accessible recreational opportunities like hiking, fishing, camping, climbing and skiing (the greatest snow on earth!). Numerous federally designated wilderness areas protect these mountains which can be reached from the city in as little time as fifteen minutes. Besides recreation and solace, the Wasatch Mountains provide water to the residents of Utah's three largest cities. Of this chain of cities, the furthest south is the Provo/Orem area, recently voted as the third and fourth best communities in which to live in the United States. Luckily for the rock climber, this area is also a limestone mecca, and within a half-hour of downtown Provo, climbers have four distinct areas to choose from.

Two dominant mountains stand at either end of the Provo/Orem region: Mount Timpanogos (which means "Sleeping Maiden") and Provo peak, both reaching a height of more than 11,000 feet. These two peaks are separated by Provo Canyon, but are joined geologically. The extensive Mississippian limestone, found throughout American Fork

Canyon, Rock Canyon, and Hobble Creek, was deposited roughly 350 million years ago, and has been folded, faulted and eroded into a snafu of rugged pinnacles, knife edge ridges, unexplored side canyons and caves.

The canyon bottoms are lush with foliage which often forms a canopy across the road. American Fork Canyon is one segment of the Alpine Scenic Loop Road, a beautiful fiesta of scenery that encompasses Mount Timpanogos and falls within the Uinta National Forest. Three hundred feet up the north slope of American Fork Canyon is the Lone Peak Wilderness Boundary; three hundred feet up the south slope is the boundary for the Timpanogos Wilderness Area. Timpanogos Cave National Monument (TCNM) focuses on a limestone cave with astounding stalactite formations.

Rock Canyon, with its dirt road closed to motorized travel and its proximity to the Brigham Young University campus, has been a haven for hikers for years. Hobble Creek is the local birthplace of limestone sport climbing and while not known for its hiking, is known for its golf course. Rock climbers, both visiting and locals, realize how lucky they are to be able to enjoy their sport surrounded by spectacular mountains and beautiful scenery.

## THE NATURE OF THE CLIMBING

This isn't the massive, clean limestone of southern France by any stretch of the imagination. To the first time visitor, the rock may look broken and rotten. And often, that is exactly what it is. But the climbing in most cases is much better than it looks in that the broken nature of the rock provides holds for the radically steep climbing, the key feature that attracts climbers. Most of the routes are vertical or greater with a variable mix of pockets and edges. Because the rock is steeper than in other areas, the holds are correspondingly bigger to achieve the same rating. So if you're tired of hanging onto micro edges, you'll find a reprieve in Utah Valley. Most of the limestone climbs are 5.11 or harder, attracting the strong and dexterous climber. Dozens of 5.13's lure the elite, where they often find their heaven in **Hell** or realize that life amid **The Projects** is tolerable. Others less skilled enjoy the climbing as well, and pushing personal limits is commonplace. A unique and healthy attitude seems prevalent in these canyons, where climbers aren't shy to encourage, share top-ropes or accept new routes.

With the exception of the quartzite at the mouth of Rock Canyon, the climbing is almost entirely protected with rappel-placed bolts that end at chain anchors. Most routes in this guide are 82 feet or shorter, and the few that are longer will hopefully be noted. Because the area has been developed by only a handful of climbers, the layout of the sport routes is consistent, with chain anchors placed well for lowering off, and bolt spacing generally uniform from route to route. Although bolts may protect a crack in American Fork and the limestone of Rock Canyon, don't expect bolts, or attempt to add bolts, to the quartzite cracks in  lower Rock Canyon.

The climbing in all of the canyons is concentrated and convenient. In American Fork, within a two mile stretch of road, you'll find buttresses stacked with routes. The approaches here, with only a few exceptions, can be done in one minute with rope in the hand and sandals on the feet. For Rock Canyon quartzite, a comfy car seat is all that is needed to belay for some routes. For the limestone we'd recommend shoes and a water bottle. And for Hobble Creek, if you're a true sport climber, maybe look at bringing bivy gear!

Holds often break off on these climbs. A route may undergo many changes in one season; therefore, ratings should not be seen as cast in stone. That jug today might be a crimper next week!

## THE ROCK CLIMATE

Surprisingly, climbing in Utah Valley is a year-round pursuit, but the best time to visit is between April and November. The months of June through October offer the most comfortable temperatures, driest rock and the most stable weather.

When a high pressure parks over northern Utah in the winter, the Salt Lake and Provo valleys suffer frequent temperature inversions which plunge the lowlands into a freezing ice fog. If you rise above this inversion layer it is often warm enough to climb on the sun-warmed, south-facing cliffs. Even during the dead of winter the **Hideaway** and **The Billboard** can be comfortable if it is a sunny day in American Fork Canyon. **The Juniper Wall**, **The Watchtower**, and the **Escape Buttress** also provide winter climbing locales, but sit much lower in the canyon and don't get enough sun to be climbable on the shortest of winter days. In Rock Canyon, check out the **Bad Bananas Wall,** the **Superbowl Wall**, and the **Buckley's Mine/Blue Wall** area. Also, if the air temperature is not too cold, the west facing quartzite walls--like **The Red Slab**, and **Ed and Terry Walls**--see some afternoon sun. Although it faces due south and sits up high, the climbing in Hobble Creek Canyon is more involved because UDOT closes the road during the winter. Those wishing to walk (or ski) will be rewarded with warmth and no crowds.

Spring is the wettest time of the year in the Wasatch, and when it rains in AF or Rock Canyon, beware. Naturally occurring rockfall greatly increases. Spring can also be frustrating because a limestone route may look dry, but may have wet pockets. Some pockets may seep late into the summer, or even all season if the summer was preceded by a particularly wet winter. Winds usually aren't a factor. However, some of the warmest winter days are accompanied by a warm south wind which precedes the next storm. Also, east winds occasionally blast down the canyons in late spring and early fall.

Summer has prolonged periods of dry, hot weather. In fact, during the summer of 1994, 20 days registered over the century mark in Provo. This shouldn't discourage the visiting climber. American Fork Canyon has a swamp-cooling effect along the stream that results in remarkably cool temperatures, perfect for those workouts on the desperates. In the dry summer heat, the stuff to run to is on the south side of the canyon: **Black Magic, Cannabis Wall**, **The Membrane**, and the north face of the **Division Wall** among others. The caves, of course, like **Hell** and **The Shining Cave**, have ample shade. In Rock Canyon, **The Zoo**, **The Cooler**, **Uncle Tom's Cabin**, **The Adjective**, and **The Projects** are good bets for cooler temperatures. Surprisingly, summer mornings at **The Projects** may require a sweater.

Fall is the magical time when climbers run about frantically, attempting to complete projects in the cool dry weather. Locally, some climbers spend the hot summer days inside at the climbing gyms, preparing for the great season ahead when the leaves change, a nip is in the air and deep blue skies stretch overhead. Autumn captures the essence of climbing in the Wasatch.

## CAMPING

There is free and unimproved camping (at the time of writing) in the North Fork of American Fork Canyon along the dirt road above and north of Tibble Reservoir. To get there, drive up American Fork Canyon (state road 92) until the road forks. Take the left fork (North Fork) towards Tibble Reservoir. Slightly less than four miles up the road, at a switch back above the reservoir, a dirt road leads off to the right (east). Follow this dirt road until the signs indicate that unimproved camping is permitted (about .3 miles).

Many choice sites exist. Of course, this could all change if climbers start trashing the area.

Swimming in the reservoir can lift your spirits after a day in **Hell.** Climbers frequently convene in the mornings at picnic areas such as **The Grey Cliffs**, for brewing up and stewing over what routes to do. For a fee of $10.00 per night, there are plenty of campsites located in Little Mill Campground (located 1.3 miles up canyon from the TCNM flagpole). Additional camping is also available at four walk-in campgrounds along the North Fork road, again at a fee of $10.00 per night.

Camping in Rock Canyon is permitted, but requires backpacking (a minimum quarter mile) with your gear. Fires are not permitted. A recent fad at **The Projects** has been to walk up in the evening, bivy at several nice sites near the base, and climb at first light.

## AMENITIES

The nearest stores to American Fork Canyon are the Kountry Korner and Kohler's Supermarket near the mouth of the canyon at the junction of Highway 92 and Highway 74. This is about 10 minutes from the climbing in AF. The Kountry Korner, known as the KK to locals, serves up burgers, fries, twinkies, and recently, Powerbars. Kohler's Supermarket offers a wide variety of food, including fresh fruit and vegetables. The town of American Fork provides the nearest restaurants. The Mi Ranchito located at 390 East State Street in American Fork dishes out the best Mexican Food. The Hogi-Yogi, located at State Street and the I-15 interchange, has some vegetarian sandwiches. In Provo, twenty minutes south, amenities flourish on every corner. (See below for recommendations.)

Rock Canyon practically spills out into suburbia with its strip malls, restaurants, shopping plazas, and ice cream parlors a tribute to unbridled growth. Located near the Brigham Young University Campus, the roads leading to Rock Canyon pass food establishments everywhere. The Good Earth Cafe at 400 west and Center Street in Provo is both a health food store and a cafe. Brackman's Bagels is near the corner of Center Street and University Street (43 East Center Street to be exact) in Provo. They sell the best bagels in Utah, and a fine cup of coffee. Cafe Thanh, located at 278 West Center Street in Provo, is the ticket for Vietnamese and Chinese cravings. Juice and Java is a great place to go for that morning cup of inspiration. They are located at 280 West and 100 North in Provo. The Olive Garden Restaurant at the corner of University Parkway and 550 West, offers pastas and fresh salads. Generally, the only commodity that may be hard to find in Provo is beer!

## SHOWERS

Without going into town, the easiest way to clean up is a quick swim in Tibble Reservoir. There are two other options for those who prefer hot water. The Mountain Springs Travel Center, located at exit 265 on I-15, offers showers for $3.00. Their phone number is (801) 489-3622. The Lehi Swimming Pool offers a swim and showers for $2.00. Their season runs from Memorial Day through Labor Day and they extend a special bonus price of $1.00 during the last two weeks. To reach the Lehi Pool take exit 281 off I-15, turn west and drive into the town of Lehi. Their address is 400 East and 200 South, Lehi.

## ROCK SHOPS

Out of chalk? Shoe blowout? Want some beta? Need a number 1 RP to protect the crux? You're in luck, it's all here, at one of the following shops.

- MOUNTAINWORKS
  95 South 300 West, Provo.
  (801) 371-0223

- HANSEN MOUNTAINEERING, INC.
  757 North State Street, Orem.
  (801) 226-7498

- IME
  3265 East 3300 South, Salt Lake City.
  (801) 484-8073

- BLACK DIAMOND
  2084 East 3900 South, Salt Lake City.
  (801) 278-0233

- REI
  3285 East 3300 South, Salt Lake City.
  (801) 486-2100

- WASATCH TOURING
  702 East 100 South, Salt Lake City.
  (801) 359-9361

## CLIMBING GYMS

Three indoor climbing gyms grace the Wasatch Front. Between them climbers can be kept busy on rainy afternoons, cold winter nights, or hot summer days: pull down, match, high step! Unfortunately, the gyms have bred a new species of climbers who are woefully ill-prepared to tackle the problems and dangers associated with climbing outdoors. Get proper instruction--Don't assume that because you are comfortable, safe, and strong inside a gym, your experience will translate to the real rock.

- ROCK GARDEN
  225 Freedom Blvd., Provo.
  (801) 375-2388

- WASATCH FRONT CLIMBING GYM
  427 W. Universal Circle (9160 S.) Sandy.
  (801) 565-3657

- ROCKREATION
  2074 East 3900 South, Salt Lake City.
  (801) 278-7473

## REST DAY DIVERSIONS

We highly recommend a tour of Timpanogos Cave. The beauty of the caverns, the unique helictites for which this cave is famous, and the stalactites, stalagmites, and draperies all combine for an incredible hour of sight seeing. In the summer, tickets for cave tours usually sell out by early afternoon, so get to the Visitor Center early or purchase your tickets in advance. (801) 756-5238

The Alpine Scenic Drive is also a beautiful tour of the alpine environment, especially in the fall when the leaves are changing. The route follows Utah 92 up American Fork Canyon and then continues into Provo Canyon on US. 189. In Provo Canyon you will see Bridal Veil Falls, a 607 foot high waterfall and very popular winter ice climbing area.

Fishing, hiking and mountain bike riding are also popular rest day activities in American Fork Canyon, Rock Canyon or the three nearby state parks. If you want to hang out at a lake or do some wind surfing, Deer Creek Reservoir near Heber City isn't too far away.

## EQUIPMENT

With very few exceptions, all you need to climb in American Fork is a rack of quickdraws, several "bail" carabiners, a brush for cleaning chalk-caked holds and a rope. 12 to 15 quickdraws are usually enough. A 55m rope is a nice luxury on some routes, and a noted necessity on others. Rope bags will keep your rope clean at the base, and some type of walking shoe is nice for the longer approaches.

The same is true for the limestone of Rock Canyon. Everything there is bolted with chain anchors. Due to the longer approaches, bringing a full water bottle is highly recommended.

A standard rack will be fine for the quartzite climbs of Rock Canyon. This should include RP type nuts, Rocks or Stoppers (at least a full set), TCU's and Friends, quickdraws, over the shoulder length runners, extra carabiners, and on a few noted routes, several small tri-cams. Historically, these routes were led using only Stoppers and Hexcentrics, so the modern-age climber should have the advantage here. However, don't assume that just because you've got the latest gadget that you'll be safe. Many of these routes are bold undertakings, and the first ascensionists were comfortable placing their own protection. Get the proper instruction to climb safe.

## ETHICS

Dave Bingham, City of Rocks guidebook author, once wrote that ethics are like toothbrushes, everyone has his or her own. While that may be true for your own personal climbing ethics, (do I grab that quickdraw or not?), it is not true when other people are affected by your judgments. Think. How are your actions going to affect climbers in the future? How will they affect hikers, picnickers, people fishing in the stream? Climbing in the Wasatch Mountains is a relaxed and enjoyable experience not because locals have an indifferent attitude towards ethics, but rather because a strict adherence to the following has existed.

The establishment of new routes on the Limestone follows these guidelines: Rappel-placed bolts are the norm. Top-roping the route beforehand to figure out the best clips and the location of the chain anchors is critical. Without this step an irrevocably frustrating route results. If the rock is too steep to safely top-rope, logically placed bolts are drilled to keep the top-roped climber from swinging out too far. Then, a few of the bolts can be moved to better clipping locations. Bad bolts or stupid clips are not tolerated. The most reliable bolts are the 3/8 or 1/2 inch by 3-1/2 inch Rawl Bolt (blue band) or Petzl chem bolts. Two bolts with washers and four link chains commonly conclude the pitch, making for an easy lower-off. A common practice now is to leave two carabiners clipped into the chains to prevent excessive wearing of the chain. The rock is hollow in places; always tap with a hammer to test it before drilling. New routes are time consuming, and expensive. If you're not up to doing a quality job, leave the route for someone else. There are plenty of established routes to climb.

Simply getting to the top of most of these routes to set up the initial top-rope is a mountaineering adventure. The cleaning can take endless hours of blue collar work, removing dirt and cobwebs from pockets, smoothing sharp calcite crystals and prying off loose flakes.

If this sounds like route manufacturing, it is, but thus far chipping or the installation of modular holds has not been tolerated. Standards have risen so fast recently that the chipped hold needed today will ruin tomorrow's test piece. When in doubt, leave it alone. Remember, **The Hell Cave** was considered impossible in 1988! Let's stop this downslide of ethics with strong public sentiment AGAINST chipped or artificial holds. Literally any face can be climbed using these tactics. What's the point?

Before drilling a new route, consider the permanent implications. Not every piece of rock has to be climbed, so why waste the time and energy to establish a bad route? What are the environmental impacts of a new route. Do birds nest nearby? Be aware that the damage you cause by establishing one route may destroy habitat for many other species. Chopping down trees at the base or trimming branches that grow against the cliff will not be tolerated, either.

A red sling or shoelace tied through the first bolt means the route hasn't been red pointed and is a project. Respect the time and effort taken for the climber to bolt and clean the lines, and stay off "their" routes until they raise a white flag or complete the route. Luckily, locals have regarded this honor system as key to their close knit community and have waited patiently, often for a year or more.

Because many of the climbs here are so hard, and aspiring climbers want the big numbers, AF and Rock Canyon see much hangdogging and working out moves bolt-to-bolt. Ultimately, the climber will try for the red point ascent. However, the real prize is to flash a given route. Therefore, the first try is often Herculean. Some of the routes flashed in this crank-conducive environment are unbelievable (see history section).

If quickdraws are left in place, respect the climber who is working on the route and leave them there.

Do not alter routes after they have been established. A good example of this is the route **Margarita,** in American Fork Canyon. Jeff Baldwin had completed the first ascent in 1990, using a difficult "rose move" to get through the crux. Sometime in the fall of 1993, someone chipped a key pocket bigger, and created a three inch foothold! How sad that a climbers ego and desire to "tick" the route ended up destroying a very unique move on a classic route for all the other climbers. Difficult moves and climbs should be seen as inspiration, not as frustration. The rock isn't an indoor gym.

## ETIQUETTE

"I don't recall your name but your manners are familiar." -Oliver Herford.

With increasing numbers of climbers using the Utah Valley canyons, overcrowding has become a serious issue. A weekend at the popular American Fork cliffs can resemble a Jackson Pollock painting: a jumble of ropes, climbers, quickdraws, belayers, and dogs.

This not only adds to the frustration of climbing at a busy wall, but increases the hazards. Hopefully, with a few pointers on conduct, tensions will be eased.

- Don't insist that everyone else enjoy your music. Have consideration for other canyon users--leave the boom boxes at home. If you are resting between attempts, let someone else get on the route. We don't own these climbs, they are here for everyone.
- If you have quickdraws on a route, be courteous and let other climbers use them. The rule here is: If quickdraws are hanging, use them.
- However, respect hanging quickdraws. Don't turn the carabiners around, or shorten the draws. Don't steal them. They aren't free booty.
- If you are top-roping a route, be aware that other climbers may wish to lead it. If there is a break in your action, step aside, pull your rope, and offer the lead to the other climbers. If they climb on your rope, they can set up a new top-rope for you.
- Avoid monopolizing a climb.  Don't climb right behind someone, or rush them.
- Communicate with climbers around you. Let them know you'd like to get on their route when they are done.
- Be patient. This is for fun, after all. If carabiners have been donated to the chain anchors, don't steal them. If there are none, consider leaving some. They reduce wear on the chains and it is far easier to replace a carabiner than a chain. It is also far easier to lower off a route.
- Top-rope off quickdraws, not off the chains. The chains are wearing out quickly.
- Let people know you are planning to pull your rope. Let them get out of the way. Yell "rope" before it starts to fall.
- This is American limestone. Holds break off. Always yell "rock," even for small pebbles falling.
- Belay, sit, or lounge out of the way, not directly under a climber.
- When you fall off your project for the umpteenth time, don't vent your anger as loud curses.
- Respect other climbers! Their 5.8 lead is just as impressive as your attempted 5.14 flash.
- HAVE FUN!

## CONSERVATION AND ACCESS

In July of 1990 a group of climbers met with representatives of the Uintah National Forest, Timpanogos Cave National Monument, the Utah County Sheriff's Department, The American Alpine Club, and the Access Fund. This meeting had positive feedback, as it seems the rangers are perfectly willing to work with climbers as long as they abide by a few simple regulations. In brief:

- No climbing at campsite 33 in Little Mill Campground when it is occupied.
- Parking for the climbing in Little Mill Campground should be on the main road, not the crowded and narrow campground road.
- No new routes in Little Mill Campground.
- Quickdraws cannot be left overnight on any route in Little Mill Campground.
- Use the path by the latrine to access the **Division Wall**. Don't walk through occupied campsites.

- Parking for **The Billboard** is limited to about five cars--use pullouts further up canyon when it is full. Try to carpool.
- No camping except in designated areas within the American Fork Canyon.
- Climbing within Timpanogos Cave National Monument and on Hanging Rock is forbidden.
- Use trails whenever possible.
- Damage to trees must be stopped or climbing privileges (esp. in Little Mill Campground) will be curtailed.
- If a ranger asks you to leave an area, please do so as quickly as possible. Maintain a good rapport with the authorities.
- Always pick up your own litter and any other garbage you come across. Pack it out.
- Respect hikers and horseback riders in Rock Canyon. Always give horses the right of way.
- Use the latrines whenever possible. When not possible, bury feces well away from trails and high-use areas and remember to pack out the toilet paper.
- Some of the approaches have super-loose talus. Try to minimize slope disturbance.
- Minimize your impact on the environment.
- Realize that other people, for many other reasons, will be enjoying these mountains.

## A NOTE ON SAFETY

It is easy to become complacent about safety while sport climbing, and several climbers have had close calls. The guilty have dropped their ropes when threading chains; assumed they were on belay when they weren't; failed to buckle their harnesses correctly; and unclipped from the "keeper" line while cleaning radically overhung routes, only to realize that they just gave themselves twenty extra feet of slack and a more than likely auger. In crowded arenas belayers are highly distracted. Stay focused! Don't let this happen to you. Pay attention to detail and always check those knots. To reiterate, be careful when the ground becomes saturated with water or during high winds, as rockfall is greatly increased.

## IN CASE OF AN EMERGENCY, PHONES ARE LOCATED AT THE TIMPANOGOS CAVE NATIONAL MONUMENT.

## HISTORY

During the late 1860's, the United States Army sent troops to Utah Valley to explore the canyons which drained into Utah Lake. Their goal was to locate gold, silver and lead deposits. The government hoped that once commercial deposits were found, hordes of "gentile" miners would flock to the area and weaken the Mormon influence. Johnston`s Army eventually located and staked numerous claims at the head of American Fork Canyon. The result was the establishment of two large communities in the canyon - Deer Creek and Forest City - in addition to a narrow-gauge railroad and a dirt road used to haul ore from Forest City. Despite all the mining activity, the Mormons remained, and the mines were closed in 1876.

Recent canyon explorers have had better luck. Their bushwacking and searching efforts are not for silver and gold, however, but for good, climbable rock. The climbing potential in Utah Valley first was discovered in the early 1970's by Dave Houser, Jim Langdon, Mark Ward and Steve Wing. These four, among others, began to climb on the obvious lines in Rock Canyon, a small drainage near the Brigham Young University campus.

At first they climbed the easier routes - **The Red Slab**, **Ed and Terry**, **The Kitchen** and the **Green Monster** - ascents considered training for the more "serious" routes in Little Cottonwood Canyon to the north. But as the climbing continued, the routes involved steeper, more technical sections of rock and the first ascensionists began to realize that Rock Canyon could provide routes as difficult as any in the state. In 1975, with the free ascents of **Piece of Meat**, **Green Monster Aid Crack** and **Edge of Night**, this realization became a matter of record.

In 1976, while living in the dorms near the mouth of Rock Canyon, Kim Miller was able to climb almost daily. Teaming up with Mark Ward, the two often would climb more than 1000 feet of rock in an afternoon. That spring, Kim made the first free ascent of **Meadow Muffin**, rated 5.12a. Kim's ascent was one of the most difficult leads of its time. Jim Knight also was establishing bold lines, and soon Utah Valley climbers were offering invitations to the Little Cottonwood crowd. Whether because of the commute or the merciless sandbagging from the locals, the Salt Lake climbers never shared the enthusiasm for Rock Canyon. By the late 70's, most of the major lines had reported ascents, and the echoes of climbers pushing their limits faded into echoes from BYU climbing classes.

During this time, Doug Hansen and partners were actively exploring the limestone of American Fork and Provo Canyons. As climbing was rooted in a "ground up" tradition, these adventures often were bold undertakings that followed rotten and crumbling cracks or unprotected faces between limestone layers. Doug and partners established many routes during this time, including a route that became known as **Free Fall** (5.8). That route was named after his friend Jerry Bransom fell off at the crux, pulled out all his anchors, and hit the ground at his friends' feet. Thinking that Jerry might be dead, his friends literally threw him in the back of a hatch back car, and drove him to the hospital. Jerry survived, but that accident remains a testament to the serious nature of limestone climbing without bolts. Never guessing that limestone would become the rock of choice for some 90's climbers, most of those routes went unreported. Doug, however, did write an article for SUMMIT magazine in 1982, in which he described the esoteric nature of climbing on limestone. He also included a section on the only way to protect the blank faces of limestone at the time - jam knots of perlon in the pockets!

By the mid 80's, Rock Canyon was being transformed by the vision of two energetic climbers -Jeff Pedersen and Boone Speed. Honing their techniques on the quartzite, they quickly moved up through the grades and began establishing their own test pieces. Having pushed the limits of Rock Canyon, they looked to other areas. Uninhibited by the "ground up" philosophy of their predecessors, they began drilling routes on rappel in Hobble Creek Canyon. These routes, which seem minor in comparison to the present-day American Fork offerings, embodied a turning point in Utah climbing history.

Teaming up with Bill Boyle and Chris Laycock, these climbers made their first discovery - that the climbing potential outside Rock Canyon was vast and exciting. Their second discovery involved the limestone itself. The rock was more solid, or at least could be cleaned to become more solid, than was originally thought. The last discovery became immediately apparent when the climbers returned to lead their routes. This rock was steep! Abandoning Hobble Creek in favor of the more accessible American Fork Canyon, they climbed the bullet hard limestone of **Black Magic** in the fall of 1988. Then they had to wait out a long winter, anticipating what the following season would bring.

With the warming of spring, Bill, Boone and Jeff created difficult routes in the sunny **Red Corners a**rea, including two rated 5.13a. From here, the crew moved on to Little Mill Campground, **The Membrane** and the **Cannabis** areas.

The energy levels of Bill, Jeff and Boone cannot be overstated. In one season, they established more than 100 new routes. Each was cleaned, bolted and led in rapid time; some of the bolting sessions were stolen during lunch breaks from work. Many of these routes were of a difficulty not seen before in northern Utah. By the late fall, the trio had moved upcanyon to the sunlit face of **The Billboard,** where Boone established **The Shining.** Rated 5.13c, this roof problem was the hardest lead of the year. They had achieved their goal. As Boone had said, an entire area, not just isolated climbs, had to be established before the area could be taken seriously.

The following year, the region was taken seriously, and climbers from all parts of the country were drawn to American Fork. Although the number of first ascents in 1990 was fewer than the year before, the standards of difficulty rose. Visiting climbers had more impact on the "new route frontier." Scott Frye established **High Water**, **Fryeing** and **Malvado.** Todd Skinner jumped on the first ascent of **Burning,** and Scott Franklin brought the roof down with his ascent of **Blow of Death (AKA Dead Souls).** J. B. Tribout made his mark on **Cannibals**, and Jim Karn left everyone awed with his flash ascent of **High Water** and **Wizards**, finishing with the **Bats Out of Hell Variation.**

Locals were not idle. Jeff Pedersen redpointed **Jug Abuse** and the awesome **Blue Mask.** Bill climbed the devious **Eating the Gun** and **This Must Be The Pickle.** Boone repeated **Blow of Death** and **Cannibals.** New walls like **The Grey Cliffs** and The Hard Rock area continued to be developed.

*Wasatch Climbing South* (as well as enthusiastic articles in both *Climbing* and *Rock and Ice* magazines) has drawn even more visitors to the limestone of American Fork. While other climbers were wrestling with pockets and edges on routes already established, the visionaries were still exploring - searching other gullies, cliffs, faces - looking to strike it rich by finding another wall or perhaps another canyon.

Ironically, that new canyon turned out to be the old familiar Rock Canyon. Only this time, climbers were looking beyond the quartzite to the limestone bands they had always considered too far from the parking lot to hike to. Chris Laylock led the first new route, **Cambrian Grey,** on what is now **Bug Barn Dance Wall**, a mere ten minute walk up a dirt road. Development was slow at first, due in a large part to the popularity of American Fork, but routes continued to be added. Dan Kohlert climbed **Ferocious** and **Atrocious,** Tom Caldwell added **The Zoo,** and Bill Ohran developed **The Cooler** and began work on **The Balcony.** Differences between American Fork and Rock Canyon were becoming apparent. In general, the rock quality in Rock Canyon is more solid and compact; though not as steep.

Then the overhanging **Projects** were discovered. Jeff Pedersen, Bill Ohran and Darren Knezek went to work, and when the dust settled, a world-class cliff had been developed. Seven routes were 5.13, and another eight were 5.12. The only other wall with such a concentration of difficult routes in the Wasatch was **The Hell Cave,** in American Fork. In an odd repeat of history, few Salt Lake locals visited Rock Canyon, leaving walls to Provo climbers to enjoy in solitude. Jeff Pedersen, Bill Ohran, and Darren Knezek practically had the canyon to themselves, a pleasant situation which remains today.

Not all new route energy focused on Rock Canyon, however. New routes in American Fork continued to be led, and first ascensionists like Jeff Baldwin, Drew Bedford, Mike Call, Gordon Douglass, Mindy Shulak, Brian Smoot and Geoff Weigand, were not merely establishing "space fillers," but were creating good hard routes on entirely new crags such as **The Hideaway, The Hideout**, and **The Escape Buttress**. In the **Hell Area**, eleven new routes were redpointed, most of these graded at 5.13d! Obviously, climbing in American Fork hasn't stagnated.

With incredible potential, climbing in Utah Valley is in its infancy. Many other canyons have been explored, look good, and put on the back burner for another day. That day may be just around the corner, or five years from now. Who knows?

The dumbfounded authors in **Lone Peak Cirque**

Photo: Libby Ellis

## KEY TO SYMBOLS USED ON TOPOGRAPHIC MAPS

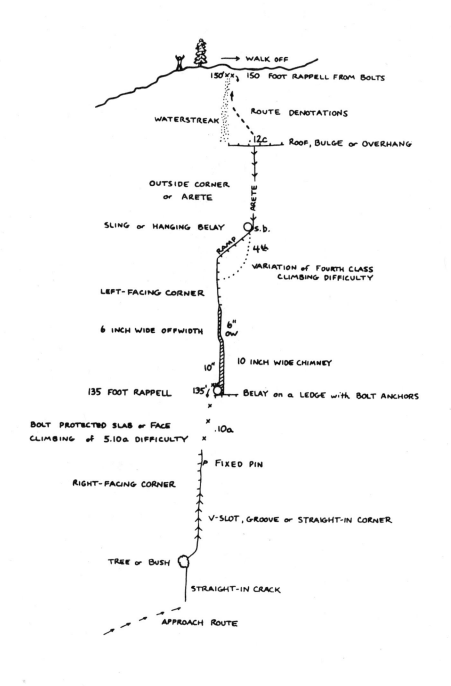

WALK OFF

150 FOOT RAPPELL FROM BOLTS

ROUTE DENOTATIONS

WATERSTREAK

ROOF, BULGE or OVERHANG

OUTSIDE CORNER or ARETE

ARETE

SLING or HANGING BELAY

RAMP

VARIATION of FOURTH CLASS CLIMBING DIFFICULTY

LEFT-FACING CORNER

6 INCH WIDE OFFWIDTH

10 INCH WIDE CHIMNEY

135 FOOT RAPPELL

BELAY on a LEDGE with BOLT ANCHORS

BOLT PROTECTED SLAB or FACE CLIMBING of 5.10a DIFFICULTY

FIXED PIN

RIGHT-FACING CORNER

V-SLOT, GROOVE or STRAIGHT-IN CORNER

TREE or BUSH

STRAIGHT-IN CRACK

APPROACH ROUTE

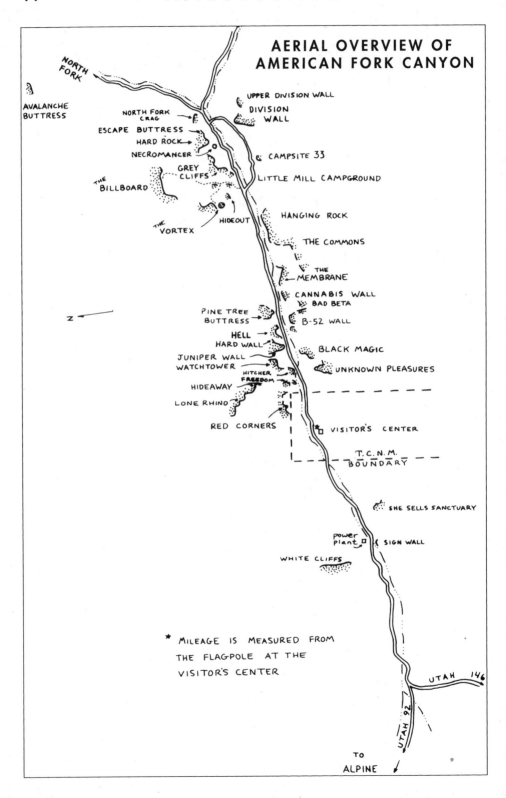

AERIAL OVERVIEW OF
AMERICAN FORK CANYON

NORTH FORK

AVALANCHE BUTTRESS

UPPER DIVISION WALL

DIVISION WALL

NORTH FORK CRAG

ESCAPE BUTTRESS

HARD ROCK

NECROMANCER

CAMPSITE 33

GREY CLIFFS

LITTLE MILL CAMPGROUND

THE BILLBOARD

HIDEOUT

HANGING ROCK

THE VORTEX

THE COMMONS

THE MEMBRANE

CANNABIS WALL
BAD BETA

PINE TREE BUTTRESS

B-52 WALL

HELL
HARD WALL

BLACK MAGIC

JUNIPER WALL
WATCHTOWER

HITCHER
FREEDOM

UNKNOWN PLEASURES

HIDEAWAY

LONE RHINO

RED CORNERS

VISITOR'S CENTER

T.C.N.M.
BOUNDARY

SHE SELLS SANCTUARY

POWER PLANT

SIGN WALL

WHITE CLIFFS

* MILEAGE IS MEASURED FROM
THE FLAGPOLE AT THE
VISITOR'S CENTER

UTAH 146

UTAH 92

TO
ALPINE

# AMERICAN FORK

THE AMERICAN FORK CANYON is a modern sport climbing area, featuring steep, challenging and innovative bolted routes. It has received widespread attention in the climbing community, and locals have worked diligently to expand the variety and quality of climbs. It is a beautiful canyon, lush with foliage, cool in the summer, and rugged with rock. The canyon cuts through the Wasatch range from the town of American Fork to the alpine slopes of Mt. Timpanogos.

## HOW TO GET THERE

From the north, take exit 287 off Interstate 15. This is the Alpine/Highland/Timpanogos Cave exit, and is located just south of "Point of the Mountain" - the gravel ridge separating Salt Lake Valley from Utah Valley. Once off I-15, drive east on Utah Highway 92; simply stay on it and you will drive directly into American Fork Canyon.
From the south, take exit 276 off Interstate 15. This is the Pleasant Grove exit. Turn right and drive east towards the mountains. Turn left on State Street. Drive north on State Street to an easy to miss intersection with Highway 146 (100 East). Turn right on 146 and follow this road all the way to the mouth of American Fork Canyon, where it joins Highway 92.

ALL MILEAGE IN AMERICAN FORK CANYON IS REFERENCED FROM THE FLAGPOLE AT THE TCNM (Timpanogos Cave National Monument).

It is possible to drive directly from American Fork Canyon to Rock Canyon without a lengthy side trip to the Interstate. Simply turn south on Highway 146 at the mouth of American Fork Canyon. Stay on 146 south until it joins Highway 89 (State Street). Turn left (south) on 89, and follow this until you come to University Mall on the left. Turn left onto University Parkway (12th So. St.) and follow the directions in the Rock Canyon Section from there.

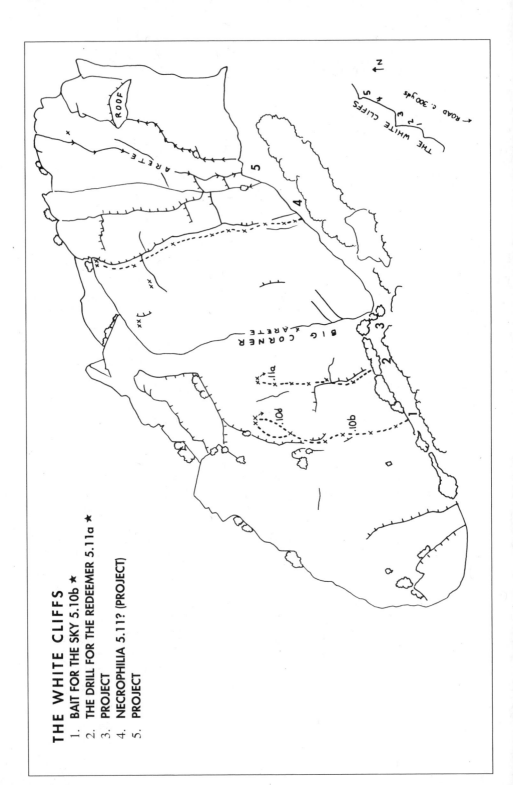

**THE WHITE CLIFFS**
1. BAIT FOR THE SKY 5.10b ★
2. THE DRILL FOR THE REDEEMER 5.11a ★
3. PROJECT
4. NECROPHILIA 5.11? (PROJECT)
5. PROJECT

## THE WHITE CLIFFS

The White Cliffs are a white east-facing cliff band rising above a gully on the north side of the road. At the time of this writing, there were numerous projects on the cliff.

APPROACH: Park on the right (south) side of the road 1.4 miles down canyon from the flagpole at TCNM. Follow a semi-trail to a talus slope. Then skip 200 yards up the talus to the cliff. The approach takes 20-25 minutes. See Aerial View page 14.

1. **BAIT FOR THE SKY 5.10b** ★ Some neat climbing initially, but gives way to sloping holds and weirdness.
   FA: Bill Boyle.
2. **THE DRILL FOR THE REDEEMER 5.11a** ★ Good climbing leads to a final dumbfounding move.
   FA: Bill Boyle.
3. **PROJECT**
4. **NECROPHILIA 5.11? (PROJECT)** Climb the crack and face in the center of the next face up from climbs 1 & 2.
5. **PROJECT**


## THE SIGN WALL

This small wall delivers one worthy route, and an approach where the car doors can scrape the base of the climb. A large sign here reads: Tourist info., Administration Office, one mile.

APPROACH: Park 1.2 miles down canyon from the TCNM flagpole at a pullout on the right (south) side of the road. The route climbs the obvious wall at the back of the pullout. See Aerial View page 14.

1. **UNKNOWN 5.11** ★ Cool moves over the roof. Blowing the fifth clip would be bad. No topo.


## SHE SELLS SANCTUARY

A real tongue twister. There is one route on this north facing arête.

APPROACH: Park at the first pullout on the left (north) side of the road, 150 feet up canyon from the power plant. This is 1.1 miles down canyon from the TCNM flagpole. Walk up the road 100 yards and look south. An arête of fine limestone is located about 300 feet up the talus, to the left (east) of a large drainage. See Aerial View page 14.

1. **SHE SELLS SANCTUARY 5.11d** ★★ Off balance climbing past six bolts to a chain anchor. A nice place to seek refuge. No topo.
   FA: Douglas Heinrich.

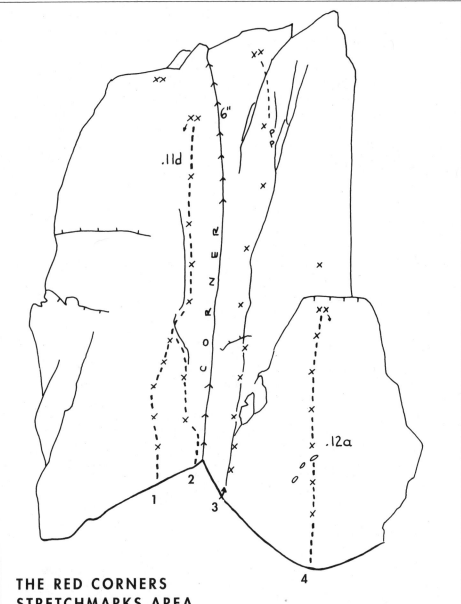

## THE RED CORNERS
## STRETCHMARKS AREA

1. SLIP SLOPIN' AWAY 5.12b/c ★★
2. RDA 5.11d ★
3. MEGADOSE 5.12c ★★
4. STRETCHMARKS 5.12a ★

## THE RED CORNERS

Just after leaving the TCNM you will see these awesome dihedrals up on the left (north) side of the road. The climbing here is unique to the canyon, involving more technical moves on edges rather than pockets.

APPROACH: This approach avoids all the hassles of the stream crossing. Park .35 miles up canyon from the TCNM flagpole at a large pullout on the left (north) side of the road. Walk up the road 200 feet to a point where the stream crosses under the road, turn left onto a small trail, and walk back down canyon 500 feet until the trail crosses a nasty talus slope. Walk up this talus for routes 14-17. Continue walking down canyon another 200 feet until a large pine tree obscures the view of **Book Of Condolences**. Walk up the large blocks 200 feet to reach routes 5-13. A trail at the base of the **Book of Condolences** area leads west another 300 feet to reach the **Stretchmarks** area (routes 1-4). See Aerial View page 14.

1.  **SLIP SLOPIN' AWAY 5.12b/c ★★** A long tribute to slopers.
    FA: Boone Speed and Bart Dahneke.
2.  **RDA 5.11d ★** The route just left of the fist crack corner.
    FA: Bart Dahneke.
3.  **MEGADOSE 5.12c ★★** Take two and call me in the morning.
    FA: Bart Dahneke.
4.  **STRETCHMARKS 5.12a ★** Less than vertical.
5.  **SISTER RAY 5.12a ★** Spectacular arête. The forth clip stumps many.
    FA: Bill Boyle.
6.  **XCESS 5.12b ★★** An exemplary example of an excellent exploit. Two ropes are required (or one 55m) to get off.
    FA: Bill Boyle.
7.  **XTENSION 5.13a ★★** The exquisite exodus extruding from X. An exotic extravaganza. Two ropes are required (or one 55m) to get off.
    FA: Boone Speed.
8.  **X 5.13a ★★★** "We're desperate, get used to it." -X lyric. A bloody brilliant route. Clip the seventh bolt and rail out right across the face.
    FA: Boone Speed.
9.  **BOOK OF CONDOLENCES 5.12b ★★★** Unrelenting stemming in the most aesthetically pleasing rock of the canyon. Style or denial!
    FA: Boone Speed and Bill Boyle.
10. **MINIMALIST (OPEN PROJECT) 5.13?** Crimpers.
11. **SILENCER 5.12d ★** Razor climbing up a mute face.
    FA: Boone Speed.
12. **CHOSS FIGHTER 5.11b** An anti-classic.
    FA: Bill Boyle.
13. **CHOSS FIRE 5.11c/d ★** Be careful, or you might get caught in it. Acceptable climbing leads to a better upper face.
    FA: Bill Boyle.

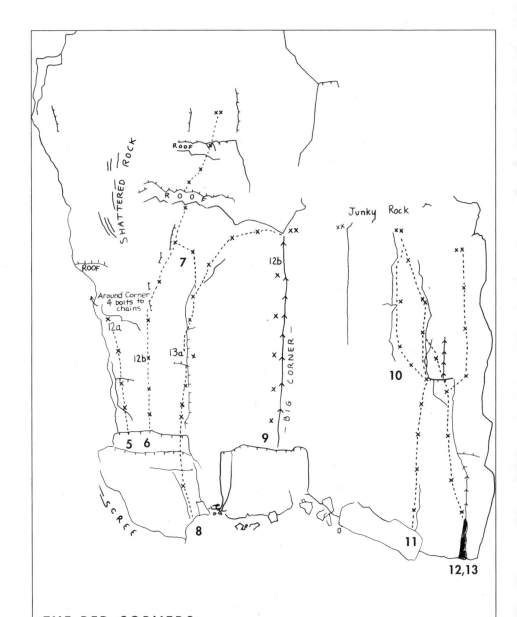

## THE RED CORNERS
## BOOK OF CONDOLENCES AREA

5. SISTER RAY 5.12a ★
6. XCESS 5.12b ★★
7. XTENSION 5.13a ★★
8. X 5.13a ★★★
9. BOOK OF CONDOLENCES 5.12b ★★★

10. MINIMALIST (OPEN PROJECT) 5.13?
11. SILENCER 5.12d ★
12. CHOSS FIGHTER 5.11b
13. CHOSS FIRE 5.11c/d ★

14. **BLUE MOON 5.11b** ★ A good 5.11b starter route.
    FA: Bill Boyle.

15. **ORGAN GRINDER 5.12a** ★ Sequential.
    FA: Boone Speed and Bill Boyle.

16. **WEANED ON A PICKLE 5.11c** ★ If the initial moves don't spit you off, the gaston
    move between the third and fourth bolts will.
    FA: Tom Caldwell.

17. **NO QUARTERS 5.13a** ★ High on the tweak meter. Many side-pulls.
    FA: Boone Speed.

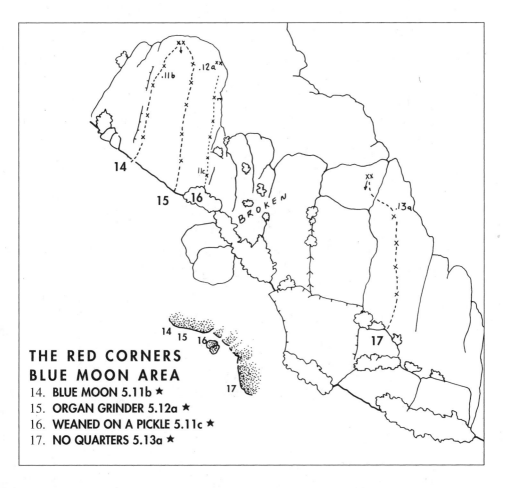

**THE RED CORNERS**
**BLUE MOON AREA**
14. **BLUE MOON 5.11b** ★
15. **ORGAN GRINDER 5.12a** ★
16. **WEANED ON A PICKLE 5.11c** ★
17. **NO QUARTERS 5.13a** ★

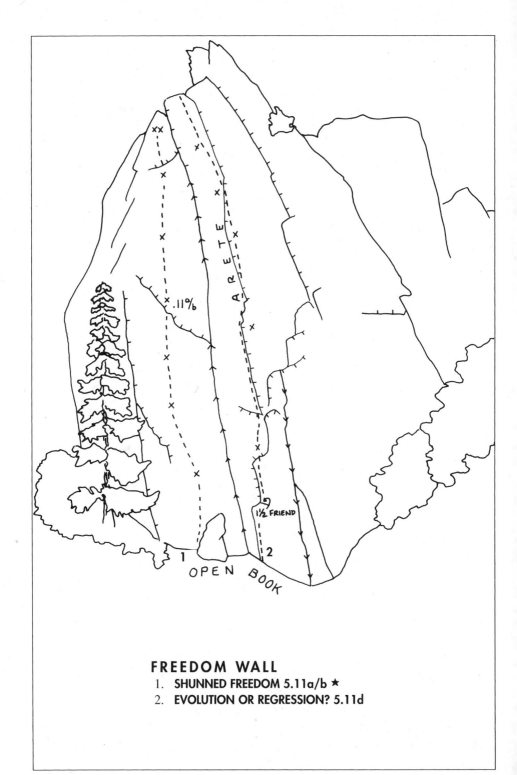

**FREEDOM WALL**
1. SHUNNED FREEDOM 5.11a/b ★
2. EVOLUTION OR REGRESSION? 5.11d

## FREEDOM WALL

The Freedom Wall is a small area with a striking open book located near the start of **The Hideaway** approach. The crag is peaceful, but the amount of climbing is limited.

APPROACH: Park .35 miles up canyon from the TCNM flagpole at a large pullout on the left (north) side of the road. Walk up the road 200 feet to a point where the stream crosses under the road, turn left onto a small trail, and walk back down canyon 200 feet. (This avoids all the hassles of the stream crossing). 50 feet west of an exposed water pipe, a small talus slope with a trail and a cairn spills out from the drainage. March up this trail for 100 feet to the first wall on the left side. See Aerial View page 14.

1. **SHUNNED FREEDOM 5.11a/b** ★ "No human being, however great, or powerful, was ever so free as a fish." -John Ruskin. A tickler that climbs the left side of the open book.
   FA: Scott Unice and Troy Chatwin.

2. **EVOLUTION OR REGRESSION? 5.11d** A one and a half Friend protects the moves to the first bolt. Some loose rock.

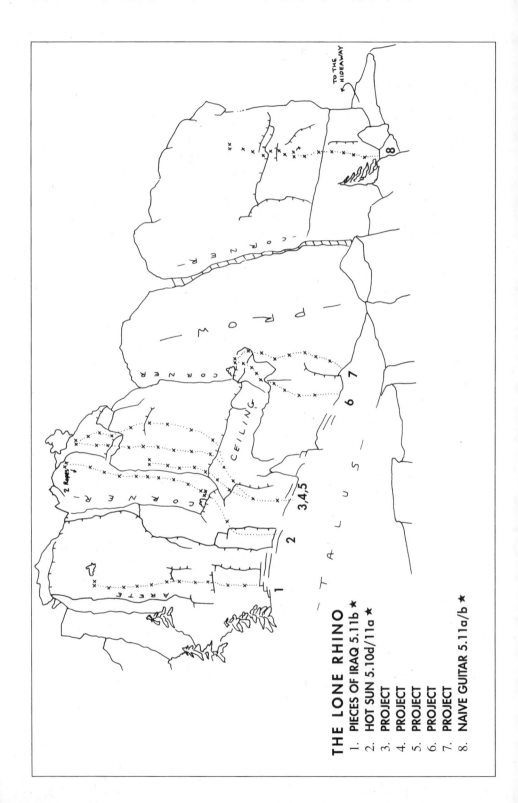

**THE LONE RHINO**
1. PIECES OF IRAQ 5.11b ★
2. HOT SUN 5.10d/11a ★
3. PROJECT
4. PROJECT
5. PROJECT
6. PROJECT
7. PROJECT
8. NAIVE GUITAR 5.11a/b ★

## THE LONE RHINO

In the fall of 1990, this area with its massive corners and faces was touted as the future of American Fork Canyon. Perhaps it was the long approach that deterred climbers, but enthusiasm for **The Lone Rhino** never ignited, and these walls are as peaceful today as ever. Perched high on the canyon's north side, and facing south and west, **The Lone Rhino** is a perfect spring, fall, and winter area.

APPROACH: Follow the approach to **The Hideaway.** From the route **Motu** at **The Hideaway,** walk west 150 feet to a ridge and a drop off. Walk up the ridge to where it meets the cliff and downclimb a twenty foot corner (5.4) to reach a ledge. Traverse west on the exposed ledge, go around the corner on the ledge system and you'll be at the base of **Naive Guitar.** Although not too difficult, this approach is exposed. Be Careful—watch for loose rock.. See Aerial View page 14.

1. **PIECES OF IRAQ 5.11b** ★ Horizontal bands lead up to a small roof. Pull the roof on better rock and follow the line of fine pockets and edges.
   FA: Bill Boyle.

2. **HOT SUN 5.10d/11a** ★ Climb to the top of the block and clip a chain link in the corner. Move up and right onto a ramp and clip into a two bolt station. At this point you can pull the rope through the first bolt, eliminating rope drag problems. Then cast off up the wall above, enjoying the edges and sidepulls. Two ropes are needed to rappel off.
   FA: Bill Boyle.

3. **PROJECT** Looks choice.

4. **PROJECT**

5. **PROJECT**

6. **PROJECT**

7. **PROJECT**

8. **NAIVE GUITAR 5.11a/b** ★ Start behind a large boulder. Climb up on horizontal striations and weird pockets to a two bolt station about half-way up the wall. Slopey. The upper route through the roofs is still a project.
   FA: Bill Boyle.

Amy Somers enjoying **Hanky Head (5.12b) The Hideaway**

Photo: James Kay

## THE HIDEAWAY

One of the newer additions to American Fork climbing, **The Hideaway** is host to a number of difficult routes, and some of the canyon's finest rock. Practically the exclusive domain of first ascensionist Jeff Baldwin, the climbs here reflect his blend of power and bouldering strength. The main wall is south facing and sits up above winter inversions which form in the valley, creating an ideal winter climbing area. Summers can be hot, although year round climbing is possible by approaching the wall in the late afternoon, or climbing in the early morning on the west facing wall. With pockets and steep rock, **The Hideaway** is a desired destination.

APPROACH: Park .35 miles up canyon from the TCNM flagpole at a large pullout on the left (north) side of the road. Walk up the road 200 feet to a point where the stream crosses under the road, turn left onto a small trail, and walk back down canyon 200 feet. (This avoids all the hassles of the stream crossing). 50 feet west of an exposed water pipe, a small talus slope with a trail and a cairn spills out from the drainage. March up the trail, passing the small **Freedom Wall,** and generally staying on the left side of the drainage. The trail is becoming more obvious with each season, so if you are bushwhacking, you're probably off route. Plan on 30-40 minutes. See Aerial View page 14.

1. **MOTU 5.10a** ★ Vertical.
   FA: Jeff Baldwin.

2. **CHARLIE DON'T SURF 5.9** ★ The easiest climb at **The Hideaway.** 6 bolts.
   FA: Bill Bender and Jeanne O'Brien.

3. **DROP ANCHOR 5.10d** ★ Drop the packs here. The warm-up climb of choice. Bigger holds than **Motu.**
   FA: Jeff Baldwin.

4. **DARK RUM 5.12b** ★★ Good slab climbing. A difficult start leads to a no hands rest, but the crux is still lurking.
   FA: Jeff Baldwin.

5. **EASTER ISLAND 5.12c** ★ A thin seam that is continuously difficult and sequential.
   FA: Jeff Baldwin.

6. **HIDEAWAY 5.12c** ★ Pockets, then edges. Technical.
   FA: Tim Roberts.

7. **SEEK AND ENJOY 5.11a** Three bolts of good pocket climbing give way to less than ideal rock.
   FA: Tim Roberts.

8. **SEACLIFF 5.10d** ★ Exciting stemming in the corner with several puzzling moves.
   FA: Jeff Baldwin.

9. **BAMBOO 5.12b** ★★★ A riot. Quality climbing up a blunt prow.
   FA: Jeff Baldwin.

10. **BON VOYAGE 5.12d** ★ A sequential journey that sends most climbers waving goodbye at the third bolt.
    FA: Jeff Baldwin.

11. **TROPICAL DEPRESSION 5.13a** ★★ A turbulent route that demands power for the bulge and endurance for the face above. May be wet in the early season.
    FA: Joe Brooks and Jeff Baldwin.

12. **CINNAMON BAY 5.12** ★★ Short and steep with a crux undercling that is often wet.
    FA: Joe Brooks.

13. **UNDERTOW 5.13a** ★ Get caught in the current with a mono move right off the
    deck.
    FA: Joe Brooks and Liz Hastings.

14. **RAZOR CLAM 5.11c/d** ★★ Stick clip the first bolt to protect the hard start. Good
    rock in the water streak.
    FA: Jeff Baldwin.

15. **LION FISH 5.12a/b** ★ Climb up and right to a pumpy crux. The hard bodies use this
    one as a warmup!
    FA: Jeff Baldwin.

16. **DRIFTING 5.12d** Stick clip the first bolt. This route feels like three separate boulder
    problems, punctuated by brief rests.
    FA: Jeff Baldwin.

17. **SEA TOMATO 5.12** ★★ Slopers for the hands and feet, followed by jug hauling.
    FA: Steve Bullock.

18. **ALCYONE 5.13a** ★★★ Simple to figure out, difficult to execute.
    FA: Jeff Baldwin.

19. **MARGARITA 5.12** ★★★ "There's booze in the blender, and soon it will render, that
    frozen concoction that helps me hang on." -Jimmy Buffet. One of the canyon's best,
    a real gem.
    FA: Jeff Baldwin.

20. **GREEN VIOLETEAR 5.12d** ★★★ A more pumpy alternative to **Margarita**. The suc-
    cessful climber will need the speed and endurance of the hummingbird that this
    route is named after.
    FA: Jeff Baldwin.

21. **FOURTEENTH ATMOSPHERE (PROJECT)**

22. **PROJECT**

23. **BLUE TYPHOON 5.13a** ★★★ Stemming up another perfect shield of rock. A tempest
    of technical and powerful moves.
    FA: Merrill Bitter.

24. **PROJECT**

25. **CITRUS 5.13b** ★★★ This climb is one continuous crux which juices even the
    strongest of fingers. **The Hideaway's** reigning test piece. Stick clip the first bolt.
    FA: Jeff Baldwin.

26. **SCREAMING LOBSTERS 5.11d** ★ Pull-ups on pockets.
    FA: Andy Ross.

Routes 27-37 are located on the West facing wall that runs parallel to the approach
gully.

27. **SERPENTINE 5.10** Move right at the pocket and join **Topaz.**
    FA: Jeff Baldwin.

28. **TOPAZ 5.10d** A cosmic thing; tricky start, relaxing finish, blue water streak.
    FA: Jeff Baldwin.

29. **CRESCENDO 5.10d** ★★ Good footwork is a prerequisite. Vertical climbing with edges and slopers for the feet.
FA: Jeff Baldwin and Paul Hodges.

30. **SUNDANCE 5.10c** ★ Casual pocket climbing is followed by a short, stumper crux.
FA: Paul Hodges and Jeff Baldwin.

31. **AFTERGLOW 5.10d** ★ Weird, yet popular, with a sporty runout between the second and third bolts. When in doubt, high step.
FA: Jeff Baldwin.

32. **PROJECT 13?** Steep.

33. **PROJECT 5.12?** Looks good.

34. **MARITIME 5.12b** ★★ Continuous pumpy climbing. Fun.
FA: Jeff Baldwin.

35. **PROJECT**

36. **HANKY HEAD 5.12b** ★ With more traffic, this is destined to become a classic.
FA: Andy Ross.

37. **BERMUDA SHORTS 5.12c** ★★ Maximum pump factor.
FA: Andy Ross.

38. **BIKINI WAX 5.11b/c** ★ Quality pocket pulling.
FA: Andy Ross.

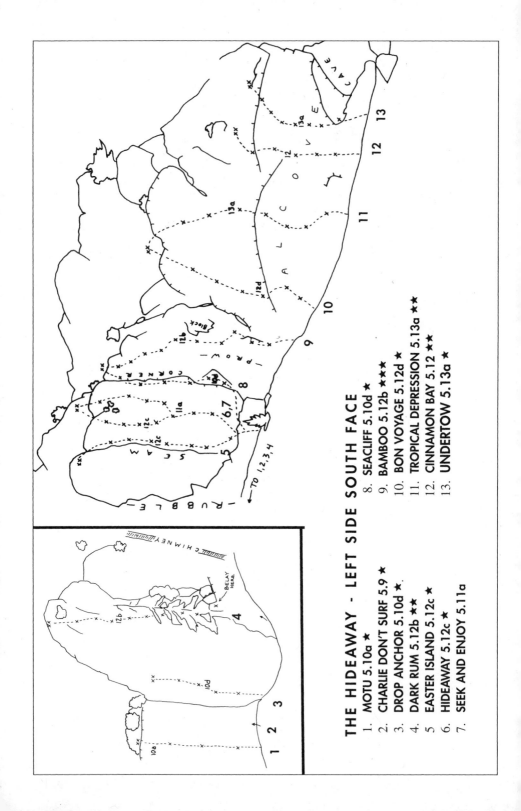

THE HIDEAWAY - LEFT SIDE SOUTH FACE

1.  MOTU 5.10a ★
2.  CHARLIE DON'T SURF 5.9 ★
3.  DROP ANCHOR 5.10d ★
4.  DARK RUM 5.12b ★★
5.  EASTER ISLAND 5.12c ★
6.  HIDEAWAY 5.12c ★
7.  SEEK AND ENJOY 5.11a

8.  SEACLIFF 5.10d ★
9.  BAMBOO 5.12b ★★★
10. BON VOYAGE 5.12d ★
11. TROPICAL DEPRESSION 5.13a ★★
12. CINNAMON BAY 5.12 ★★
13. UNDERTOW 5.13a ★

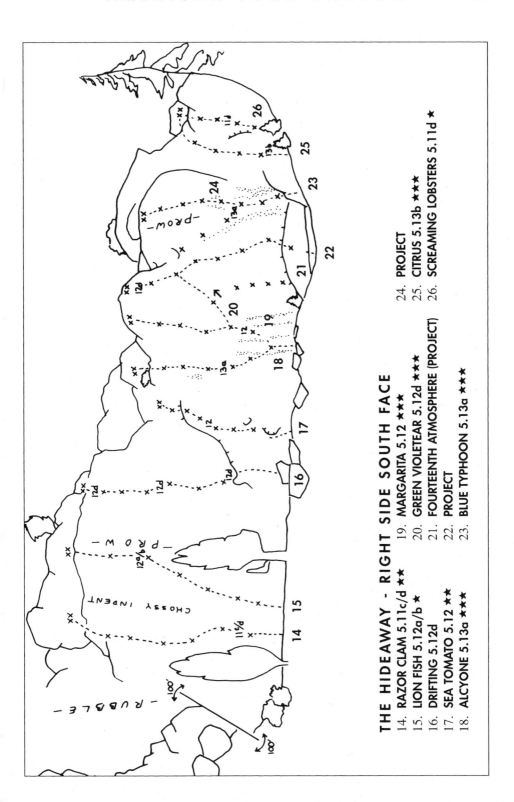

## THE HIDEAWAY - RIGHT SIDE SOUTH FACE

14. RAZOR CLAM 5.11c/d ★★
15. LION FISH 5.12a/b ★
16. DRIFTING 5.12d
17. SEA TOMATO 5.12 ★★
18. ALCYONE 5.13a ★★★

19. MARGARITA 5.12 ★★★
20. GREEN VIOLETEAR 5.12d ★★★
21. FOURTEENTH ATMOSPHERE (PROJECT)
22. PROJECT
23. BLUE TYPHOON 5.13a ★★★

24. PROJECT
25. CITRUS 5.13b ★★★
26. SCREAMING LOBSTERS 5.11d ★

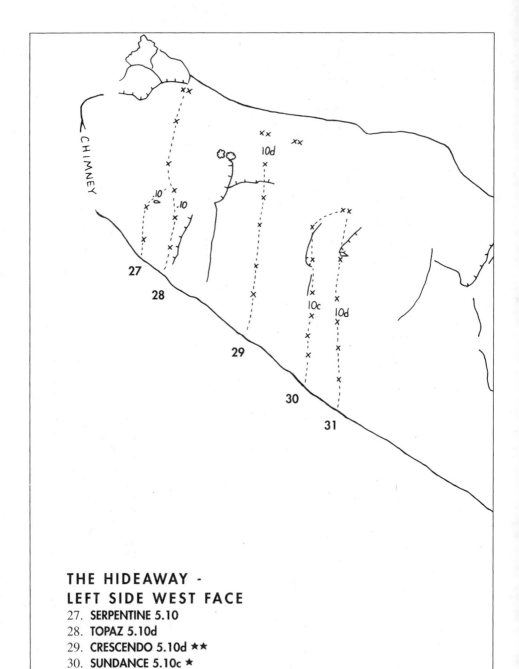

**THE HIDEAWAY -
LEFT SIDE WEST FACE**

27. SERPENTINE 5.10
28. TOPAZ 5.10d
29. CRESCENDO 5.10d ★★
30. SUNDANCE 5.10c ★
31. AFTERGLOW 5.10d ★

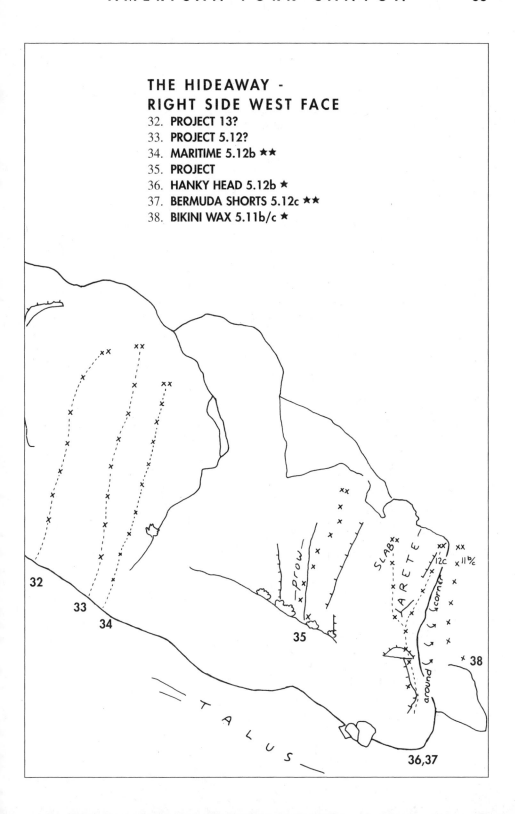

THE HIDEAWAY -
RIGHT SIDE WEST FACE
32. PROJECT 13?
33. PROJECT 5.12?
34. MARITIME 5.12b ★★
35. PROJECT
36. HANKY HEAD 5.12b ★
37. BERMUDA SHORTS 5.12c ★★
38. BIKINI WAX 5.11b/c ★

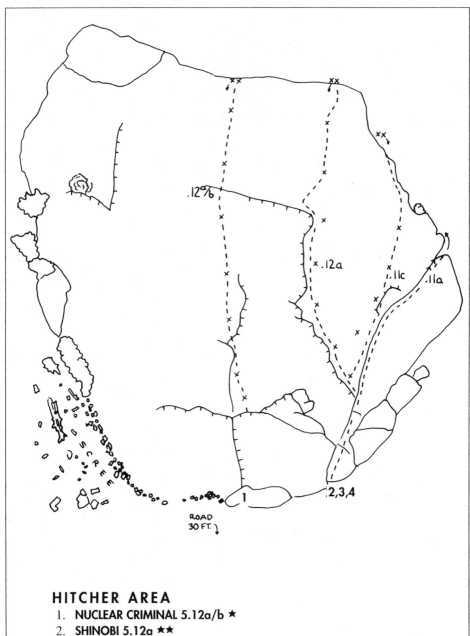

## HITCHER AREA
1. NUCLEAR CRIMINAL 5.12a/b ★
2. SHINOBI 5.12a ★★
3. HITCHER 5.11c ★
4. CHERNOBYL 5.11a

## HITCHER AREA

This small outcrop has four routes that overhang in a big way. A 20 second approach and good rock add to the value. **The Hitcher** area is directly north across the road from the **Black Magic** parking.

APPROACH: Park .5 miles up canyon from the TCNM flagpole (or .15 miles down canyon from **Hell's** parking area), at a small pullout on the right (south) side of the road. Walk down canyon 50 feet and cross the road. The routes are located on the wall 30 feet off the road. See Aerial View page 41.

1. **NUCLEAR CRIMINAL 5.12a/b ★** "The release of atomic energy has changed everything except our way of thinking and thus we are being driven unarmed towards a catastrophe." -Albert Einstein. You may experience meltdown in several places.
   FA: Bill Boyle.

2. **SHINOBI 5.12a ★★** Some cranker moves in a corner thwart the masses.
   FA: Bill Boyle and Boone Speed.

3. **HITCHER 5.11c ★** Climb the crack and face on the right side. This is still American Fork's big time sandbag!
   FA: Boone Speed and Bill Boyle.

4. **CHERNOBYL 5.11a** The crack on the right side has been led with gear. Sharp. Bring medium nuts and TCUs.
   FA: Bret and Stuart Ruckman.

Mindy Shulak gets twisted on **The Helix [5.12b] Black Magic Cave**

Photo: James Kay

## BLACK MAGIC CAVE

Some of the canyon's finest rock, and some of the canyon's wildest routes are to be found on these black, shady walls. Cool in the summer, quick approach, stacks of good routes, all boil down to a rock wizard's potion for fun.

APPROACH: Park .5 miles up canyon from the TCNM flagpole (or .15 miles down canyon from Hell's parking), at a small pullout on the right (south) side of the road. Walk down canyon 50 feet, cross the stream on a log jam and head up the slope 200 feet to the austere cave. During high-water, walk east up the road 200 feet from the parking area, cross the stream on a pipe bridge, turn right and follow a good trail back down canyon. Several quick up and down sections deposit the climber at a talus slope. Walk down this talus slope a short distance to the base of **Problem Child**. See Aerial View page 41.

1. **ABANDONED PROJECT** Cruiser climbing leads to a blank finish. This may have seen a lead at this point.

2. **PROBLEM CHILD 5.12c ★★** Well worth an attempt...or two.
   FA: Jeff Pedersen.

3. **THE PRICE IS RIGHT 5.11d ★** Climb the first four bolts of **Problem Child**, cut right past a new bolt, and finish on **Distraction.**
   FA: Gordon Douglass.

4. **DISTRACTION 5.11c ★** Leftward leanings on good rock.
   FA: Boone Speed and Bill Boyle.

5. **STAY ON THE PORCH 5.11c/d ★** Weirdness on small edges and slopers. A surprisingly good route.
   FA: Bill Boyle and Boone Speed.

6. **BLACK MAGIC 5.12b/d ★★** "I've been forty years discovering that the queen of all colours is black." -Auguste Renoir. Pockets disappear into slopers on some of the finest stone in the canyon. Totally height dependent crux. This was the first sport route in the canyon.
   First TR: Steve Gibb.
   FA: Boone Speed.

7. **TULSA 5.12b ★** A cross country journey. A wicked slab reaches the bulge and the headwall above. There is a scary block that if knocked loose would land on the belayer. Some say it is loose, some say it is solid...
   FA: Vince Adams.

8. **SIMIAN 5.13b/c ★★** A radical route fit for apes. Start at the prominent blue streak, climb the slab, then enter the horizontal world.
   FA: Jeff Pedersen.

9. **HELIX 5.12b ★★★** A twister that is one of the most unique outings around. Start on the east wall of the cave, 20 feet right of **Simian**. Clip nine bolts in a clockwise helix, spiraling up to two enviro-hangers in the big hole at the apex of the cave's interior.
   FA: Gordon Douglass and Mindy Shulak.

10. **TRUE LIES 5.12c ★★** "And, after all, what is a lie? `Tis but the truth in masquerade.'" -Lord Byron. Climb 30 feet of rubble above the obnoxious peace-sign graffiti. Climb pockets out a horizontal shield to the right, and then straight up to the anchor. Five bolts. A truly burly route.
    FA: Gordon Douglass and Mindy Shulak.

11. **LOST BOYS (PROJECT)** Wild looking cave project that climbs straight above **Lost Boys** graffiti on the right (west) side of the cave. Joins **Helix** for the last two bolts.

12. **PROJECT** A two bolt variation that cuts left at the fourth bolt of **Orogeny.**

13. **PROJECT** Climb **Orogeny** to the sixth bolt, then slide left and continue up the face.

14. **OROGENY 5.12a ★★★** Subduction leads to orogeny. The dirty start hardly detracts from the bullet-hard face above.
    FA: Bill Ohran.

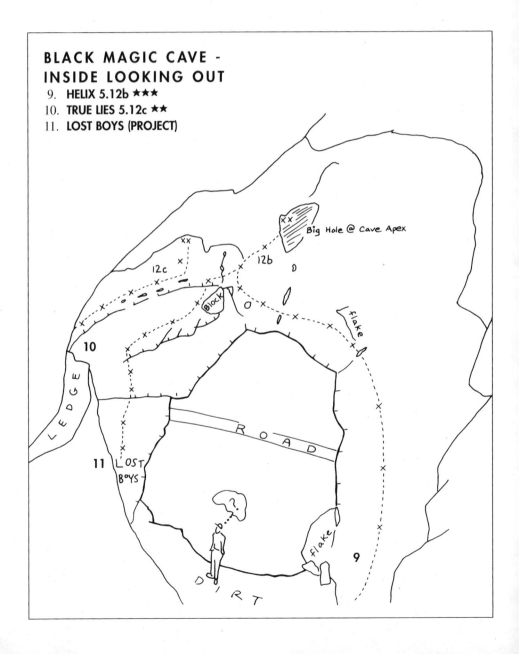

**BLACK MAGIC CAVE -
INSIDE LOOKING OUT**
9. **HELIX 5.12b ★★★**
10. **TRUE LIES 5.12c ★★**
11. **LOST BOYS (PROJECT)**

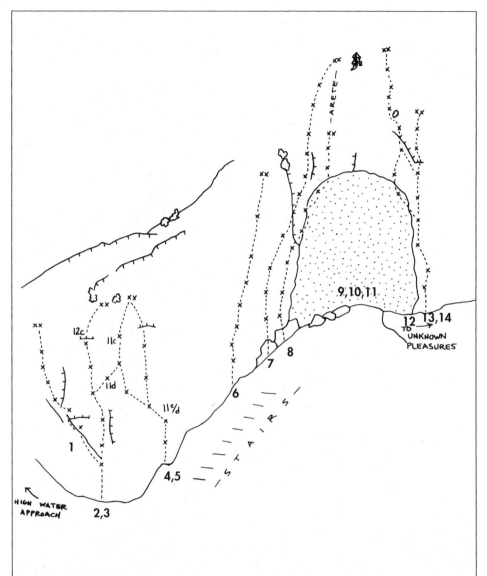

## BLACK MAGIC CAVE

1. ABANDONED PROJECT
2. PROBLEM CHILD 5.12c ★★
3. THE PRICE IS RIGHT 5.11d ★
4. DISTRACTION 5.11c ★
5. STAY ON THE PORCH 5.11c/d ★
6. BLACK MAGIC 5.12b/d ★★
7. TULSA 5.12b ★
8. SIMIAN 5.13b/c ★★
9. HELIX 5.12b ★★★
10. TRUE LIES 5.12c ★★
11. LOST BOYS (PROJECT)
12. PROJECT
13. PROJECT
14. OROGENY 5.12a ★★★

Malcolm (H.B.) Matheson stretching for **Black Magic [5.12 b/d]** **Black Magic Cave**

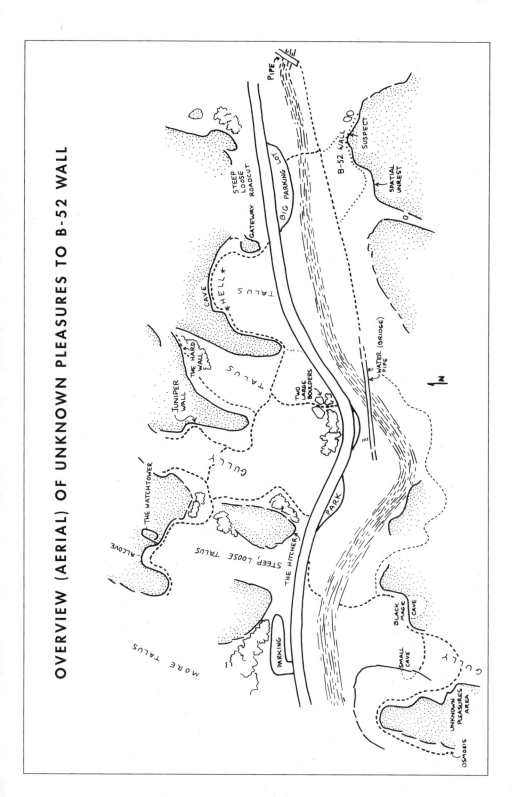

OVERVIEW (AERIAL) OF UNKNOWN PLEASURES TO B-52 WALL

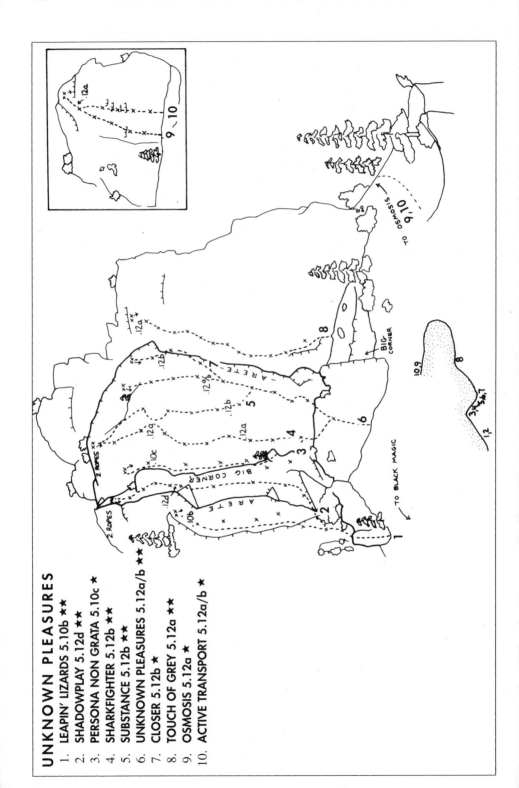

## UNKNOWN PLEASURES

1. LEAPIN' LIZARDS 5.10b ★★
2. SHADOWPLAY 5.12d ★★
3. PERSONA NON GRATA 5.10c ★
4. SHARKFIGHTER 5.12b ★★
5. SUBSTANCE 5.12b ★★
6. UNKNOWN PLEASURES 5.12a/b ★★
7. CLOSER 5.12b ★
8. TOUCH OF GREY 5.12a ★★
9. OSMOSIS 5.12a ★
10. ACTIVE TRANSPORT 5.12a/b ★

## UNKNOWN PLEASURES

This cliff is above and west of the **Black Magic Cave** and offers a high concentration of good, long routes on vertical to slightly overhanging rock. These walls are shady in the summer, rarely crowded, and provide much pleasure.

APPROACH: Follow the **Black Magic Cave** approach. From the cave, simply continue west on a trail angling up and right across talus to the cliff. To reach the **Osmosis** area, continue walking on the trail past the **Unknown Pleasures** area as it traverses a terrace around to the west side of the formation. It is three minutes from **Unknown Pleasures.** See Aerial View page 41.

1. **LEAPIN' LIZARDS 5.10b** ★★ The start is cleaning up, and once in the corner the stemming is good and airy.
   FA: Bill Boyle.

2. **SHADOWPLAY 5.12d** ★★ Start as for **Leapin' Lizards**, but set out right. A specter of sidepulls and sporty runouts. Bring two ropes or one 55 meter to get off.
   FA: Jeff Pedersen.

3. **PERSONA NON GRATA 5.10c** ★ The long stemming corner; the main feature on the wall.
   FA: Bill Boyle.

4. **SHARKFIGHTER 5.12b** ★★ Predacious. The tasty bolt line right of the corner. Bring two ropes or one 55 meter to get off.
   FA: Bill Boyle.

5. **SUBSTANCE 5.12b** ★★ Climb **Unknown Pleasures** past the overhanging pocket moves, then blast out left to encounter **Substance** abuse.
   FA: Boone Speed, Jeff Pedersen

6. **UNKNOWN PLEASURES 5.12a/b** ★★ Power up the initial moves and continue on thinner holds to a pumping finale.
   FA: Jeff Pedersen.

7. **CLOSER 5.12b** ★ A strange diversion from **Unknown Pleasures**. A heinous runout plays havoc with the composure of most climbers.
   FA: Jeff Pedersen, 1990.

8. **TOUCH OF GREY 5.12a** ★★ Strive for a touch of grace. Miles of excellent climbing leads to one final hurdle. 12 bolts. A little harder if you're shorter.
   FA: Steve Bleyl.

9. **OSMOSIS 5.12a** ★ A cozy area on the west side of the **Unknown Pleasures** wall offers two routes. This is the left line. The final clip is difficult.
   FA: Jeff Pedersen and Steve Bleyl.

10. **ACTIVE TRANSPORT 5.12a/b** ★ The more overhanging right line that shares the crux with **Osmosis.**
    FA: Jeff Pedersen.

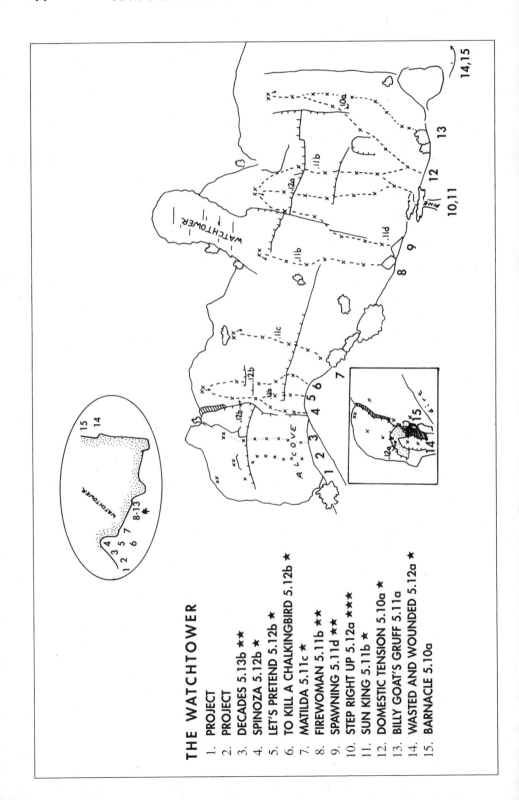

## THE WATCHTOWER

1. PROJECT
2. PROJECT
3. DECADES 5.13b ★★
4. SPINOZA 5.12b ★
5. LET'S PRETEND 5.12b ★
6. TO KILL A CHALKINGBIRD 5.12b ★
7. MATILDA 5.11c ★
8. FIREWOMAN 5.11b ★★
9. SPAWNING 5.11d ★★
10. STEP RIGHT UP 5.12a ★★★
11. SUN KING 5.11b ★
12. DOMESTIC TENSION 5.10a ★
13. BILLY GOAT'S GRUFF 5.11a
14. WASTED AND WOUNDED 5.12a ★
15. BARNACLE 5.10a

## THE WATCHTOWER

Facing south, **The Watchtower** is a good late fall and early spring area. The climbing here is almost devoid of pockets, yet edges abound. These fun routes are justifiably popular.

APPROACH: Park at a small pullout on the right side of the road .5 miles up canyon from the TCNM flagpole (.15 miles down canyon from **Hell's** parking). Walk up canyon 200 feet until some big boulders on the left are just visible through the trees. Follow a trail that starts at the boulders and heads up the slope to a junction. Turn left and follow the trail around the base of a buttress (**Juniper Wall**). Continue traversing left across the top of a talus slope, then make a nasty scramble up loose talus to the cliff. See Aerial View page 41.

1. **PROJECT**

2. **PROJECT**

3. **DECADES 5.13b** ★★ "We must use time as a tool, not as a couch." -John F. Kennedy. Six bolts of cranking madness. Climbing similar to **Hell.**
   FA: Jeff Pedersen.

4. **SPINOZA 5.12b** ★ The corner in the back of the alcove. Stemming, layaways, and precise footwork are the price for this ride. FA: Bill Boyle.

5. **LET'S PRETEND 5.12b** ★ A two bolt direct start to **Spinoza**. Bouldery. Pretending that holds really do exist is more than helpful.
   FA: Bill Boyle and Boone Speed.

6. **TO KILL A CHALKINGBIRD 5.12b** ★ Turn two torturing roofs to a pseudo slab.
   FA: Bill Boyle.

7. **MATILDA 5.11c** ★ The arête has devious face moves and an awkward roof.
   FA: Bill Boyle.

8. **FIREWOMAN 5.11b** ★★ Smoke on the horizon? Well protected, with a tricky second clip and an athletic finish.
   FA: Doug Heinrich and Steve Bullock.

9. **SPAWNING 5.11d** ★★ Climbing in the center of the south face. Follow indistinct cracks, which require a fingerlock (or two).
   FA: Bill Boyle.

10. **STEP RIGHT UP 5.12a** ★★★ ...and enjoy. Great face climbing with two small roofs leading directly to the chains. "Full-on killer finish" -Boone Speed.
    FA: Bill Boyle.

11. **SUN KING 5.11b** ★ Fun in the sun for the seasoned 11b climber.
    FA: Doug Heinrich.

12. **DOMESTIC TENSION 5.10a** ★ Diagonal to the right past five bolts on touchy terrain. Cryptic moves on the traverse.
    FA: Tom Hansen.

13. **BILLY GOAT'S GRUFF 5.11a** A brusque route on the far right side of the wall.
    FA: Bill Boyle.

The following two routes are located on the east face of **The Watchtower**, across the gully and up from the **Juniper Wall**.

14. **WASTED AND WOUNDED 5.12a** ★ The roof is a pumper boulder problem, followed
    by perplexing pocket pulling.
    FA: Bill Boyle.

15. **BARNACLE 5.10a** Climb the ugly-looking crack in the corner via stems and face
    climbing.

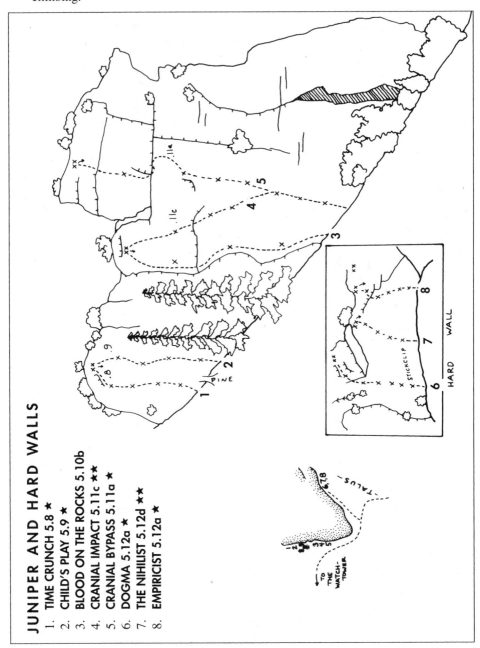

**JUNIPER AND HARD WALLS**
1. TIME CRUNCH 5.8 ★
2. CHILD'S PLAY 5.9 ★
3. BLOOD ON THE ROCKS 5.10b
4. CRANIAL IMPACT 5.11c ★★
5. CRANIAL BYPASS 5.11a ★
6. DOGMA 5.12a ★
7. THE NIHILIST 5.12d ★★
8. EMPIRICIST 5.12a ★

## JUNIPER AND HARD WALLS

**Juniper Wall** offers several routes in the moderate range in addition to fashionable crankers. The climbs here are dominated by edges and sidepulls. The **Juniper Wall** faces west and is a nice afternoon area on cold days. The **Hard Wall**, a short mini-cave facing southeast between the **Juniper Wall** and **Hell,** necessitates strong fingers and stronger forearms.

APPROACH: Park at a small pullout on the right side of the road .5 miles up canyon from the TCNM flagpole (.15 miles down canyon from Hell's parking). Walk up the road 200 feet until several big boulders are just visible through the trees on the left. Head up a trail that starts at the boulders and leads to a junction. From here **Hard Wall** is straight above this point; however, for **Juniper Wall** traverse left (west) on the trail 200 feet and go around the corner to the west-facing wall above. See Aerial View page 41.

1. **TIME CRUNCH 5.8** ★ "The surest poison is time." -R.W. Emerson. A short route behind the pine tree. Less than vertical, this is one of the easier offerings in the canyon.
   FA: Tom Hansen and Scott Unice.

2. **CHILD'S PLAY 5.9** ★ The route just right of the pine tree. A nondescript route that sees a lot of traffic.
   FA: Tom Hansen and Scott Unice.

3. **BLOOD ON THE ROCKS 5.10b** Loose rock.
   FA: Ralph Mitchell and Bill Boyle.

4. **CRANIAL IMPACT 5.11c** ★★ Start with **Cranial Bypass** and move left after the third bolt. Excellent climbing up high.
   FA: Bill Boyle.

5. **CRANIAL BYPASS 5.11a** ★ Bypass the blank section above the sixth bolt by climbing to the right. Failure to do so could create a real blockage.
   FA: Bill Boyle and Scott Unice.

The following routes are located on the Hard Wall. This is a short southeast facing wall between the Juniper Wall and Hell.

6. **DOGMA 5.12a** ★ A code of beliefs requiring two cruxes. Stick-clip the first bolt.
   FA: Bill Boyle.

7. **THE NIHILIST 5.12d** ★★ Anarchy? Stick-clip the first bolt. Many slopers and crimp holds are to be found on this American Fork stroll.
   FA: Boone Speed.

8. **EMPIRICIST 5.12a** ★ Experiment on the rightmost route.
   FA: Bill Boyle.

David Hayes leading **Hell [5.13a/b] Hell Cave**

## HELL

The **Hell** area, destination for many of the world's finest rock climbers, is a dark cave with two radically overhanging flanks. Once dismissed as impossible, **Hell** now sports the greatest concentration of difficult routes in Utah. Even with the dramatic increase in climbing standards recently, **Hell** is still one of the most challenging areas in the United States.

The cave is known to non-climbers and Provo teenagers as **Dance Hall Cave,** and it is easy to imagine the partying that has taken place in this eerie spot. Now, with large bolts, quickdraws dangling, and climbers contorting themselves overhead, the atmosphere is vastly different. Big holds abound—pockets, edges, sidepulls—holds which require unique body positions. Climbing here is often a horizontal experience. The cave has bred a microcosm of mutant climbers, able to hang upside down for preposterous periods of time. Most climbers are hesitant when they first enter **Hell**, but if you're in a hurry to get strong, there is no better place to go. The Devil's price for a redpoint is steeeep!

APPROACH: Park at the **Hell** parking area .65 miles up canyon from the TCNM flagpole. At the lowest point of the parking area (west end), cross the road and walk down canyon twenty feet. A trail here heads north, winds up a slope and ends at the hidden **Hell Cave**. See Aerial View page 41.

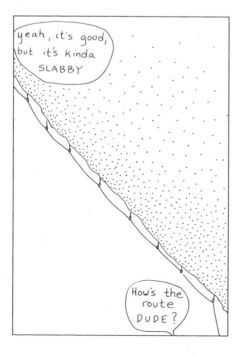

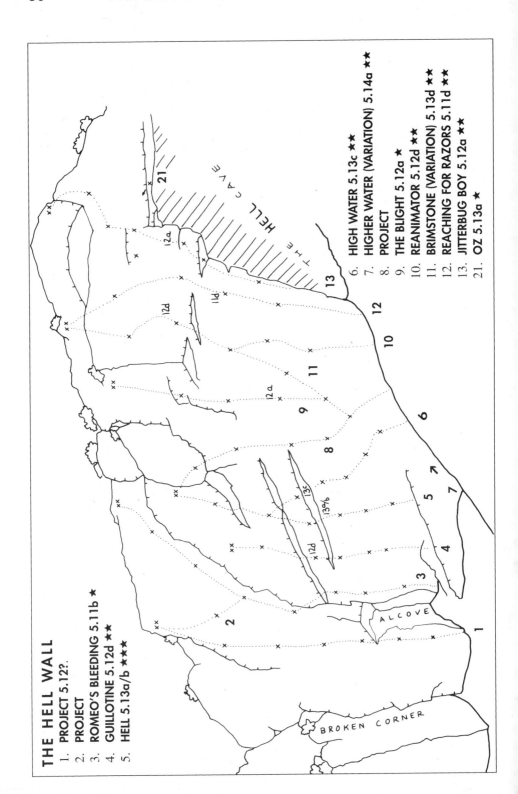

THE HELL WALL
1. PROJECT 5.12?.
2. PROJECT
3. ROMEO'S BLEEDING 5.11b ★
4. GUILLOTINE 5.12d ★★
5. HELL 5.13a/b ★★★

6. HIGH WATER 5.13c ★★
7. HIGHER WATER (VARIATION) 5.14a ★★
8. PROJECT
9. THE BLIGHT 5.12a ★
10. REANIMATOR 5.12d ★★
11. BRIMSTONE (VARIATION) 5.13d ★★
12. REACHING FOR RAZORS 5.11d ★★
13. JITTERBUG BOY 5.12a ★★
21. OZ 5.13a ★

## THE HELL WALL

This wall forms the west flank of the **Hell Cave**. A popular boulder traverse begins at **Hell** and moves up-slope to **Jitterbug Boy. (V 7/8)**

1. **PROJECT 5.12?** Nearing completion.

2. **PROJECT** Crosses the gap between the project on the left side of the wall and **Romeo's Bleeding**???

3. **ROMEO'S BLEEDING 5.11b** ★ Awkward and hard, this route climbs the prominent corner on the left side of the wall. The climbing doesn't end at **Guillotine's** anchors, but continues up past two more bolts to a higher set of chains.
FA: Bill Boyle.

4. **GUILLOTINE 5.12d** ★★ Heads will roll on this cutting-edge test piece. A bouldery, less difficult version of **Hell.**
FA: Tim Hannig.

5. **HELL 5.13a/b** ★★★ " I hold it to be the inalienable right of anybody to go to hell in his own way." -Robert Frost. A powerful classic. A barrage of strange sequences characterizes this, the progenitor of the mega-pumps.
FA : Boone Speed.

6. **HIGH WATER 5.13c** ★★ Flash the flood of cruxes to join the upper portion of **Hell.**
FA: Scott Frye.

7. **HIGHER WATER (VARIATION) 5.14a** ★★ Climb the boulder traverse beginning under **Hell** and moving rightward to join and finish **High Water.**
FA: Dale Goddard.

8. **PROJECT** Bad bolts, bad rock.

9. **THE BLIGHT 5.12a** ★ Feast or famine on small edges. Deceptive, with a hard clip.
FA: Bill Boyle.

10. **REANIMATOR 5.12d** ★★ A crash course on crimp holds.
FA: J.B. Tribout.

11. **BRIMSTONE (VARIATION) 5.13d** ★★ Start at the boulder traverse beginning under **Hell.** Traverse rightward through the first and second bolts of **The Blight**, up past a new bolt to join **Reanimator** at its third bolt. Finish on **Reanimator**. A good fingery route.
FA: Geoff Weigand.

12. **REACHING FOR RAZORS 5.11d** ★★ The name says it all. A popular route that cuts you down.
FA: Bill Boyle.

13. **JITTERBUG BOY 5.12a** ★★ Scrunch to the right in a series of confusing and contorting moves.
FA: Bill Boyle.

## HELL CAVE

This dark, moody cave is home to two boulder traverses that are worthy of note. **The Peace, Dog, Beer Traverse** begins under **Linus** and climbs rightward to the stem at the very back of the cave (**V8**). **The Fuck Me Traverse**, named after the graffiti it crosses, starts at **Cannibals** and moves up slope to **Wizards (V4)**.

14. **WASATCH REALITY 5.12a** ★ Stroll up the ungainly crack. Sharp.
    FA: Bill Boyle.

15. **BURNING 5.13b** ★★★ "No spectacle is nobler than a blaze." -Dr. Samuel Johnson. A blitzkrieg of delirious moves out a shelf to join **Wasatch Reality**. Shuffle right for two more bolts to clip the fixed carabiners.
    FA: Todd Skinner.

16. **LINUS 5.13c** ★★ No security blanket here. Start at the back of the cave near the peace, dog, beer, cave graffiti. Climb past four bolts and the infamous "snake eyes," to cross **Burning** and finish on **Wasatch Reality's** fourth bolt.
    FA: Mike Beck.

17. **FRYEING 5.13c** ★★★ Are you fit to be fried? A more difficult variation to **Burning**. After the sixth bolt on **Burning**, cut right to the seventh bolt of **Cannibals**, and keep sizzling through the crux of **Wizards**. Finish on **Bats Out Of Hell**.
    FA: Scott Frye.

18. **PROJECT 5.14?** A three bolt direct start to **Cannibals**.

19. **CANNIBALS 5.13d/.14a** ★★★ A must for the power hungry. Ignore the jug at the sixth bolt on **Burning**, and pull the **Bats Out Of Hell** roof. As with **Wizards**, you may want to tape your hands.
    FA: J.B. Tribout.

20. **MELTING 5.12d/.13a** ★★★ Climb up **Wizards** to the third bolt, angle left to the fifth bolt on **Cannibals**, continue left to the eighth bolt on **Burning** and finish on **Burning.** This is the most popular route in the cave.
    FA: Boone Speed.

21. **OZ 5.13a** ★ Climb **Melting** to the wide undercling. Traverse left past four bolts to the top of **Reaching For Razors**. Some rope drag is inevitable.

22. **WIZARDS 5.13b** ★★★ Route magicians defy gravity after the fifth bolt. Handjams in American Fork? Taping is a good idea.
    FA: Boone Speed.

23. **BATS OUT OF HELL 5.12d** ★ Choose your route to the **Wizards** anchor, then continue past two more bolts until your eyes bulge.

24. **I SCREAM (OPEN PROJECT) 5.14?**

25. **SIDE SHOW BOB'S 5.13b/c** ★★ A demanding start and a difficult roof problem (bad feet, holds slope the wrong way, etc.) are packed into this shortie. Stick clip the second bolt.
    FA: Mike Call.

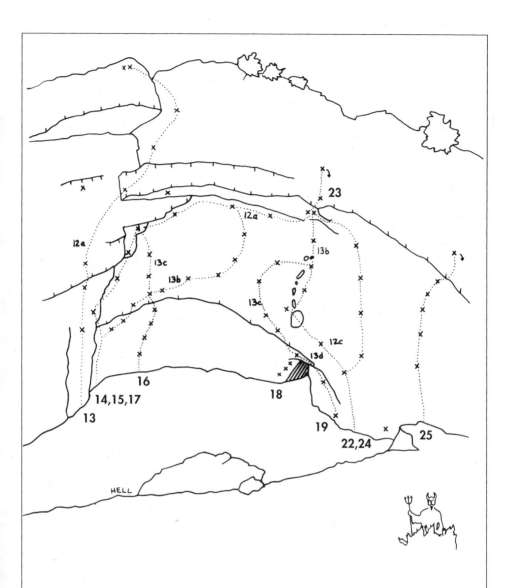

## HELL CAVE

13. **JITTERBUG BOY 5.12a** ★★
14. **WASATCH REALITY 5.12a** ★
15. **BURNING 5.13b** ★★★
16. **LINUS 5.13c** ★★
17. **FRYEING 5.13c** ★★★
18. **PROJECT 5.14?**
19. **CANNIBALS 5.13d/.14a** ★★★
20. **MELTING 5.12d/.13a** ★★★
21. **OZ 5.13a** ★
22. **WIZARDS 5.13b** ★★★
23. **BATS OUT OF HELL 5.12d** ★
24. **I SCREAM (OPEN PROJECT) 5.14?**
25. **SIDE SHOW BOB'S 5.13b/c** ★★

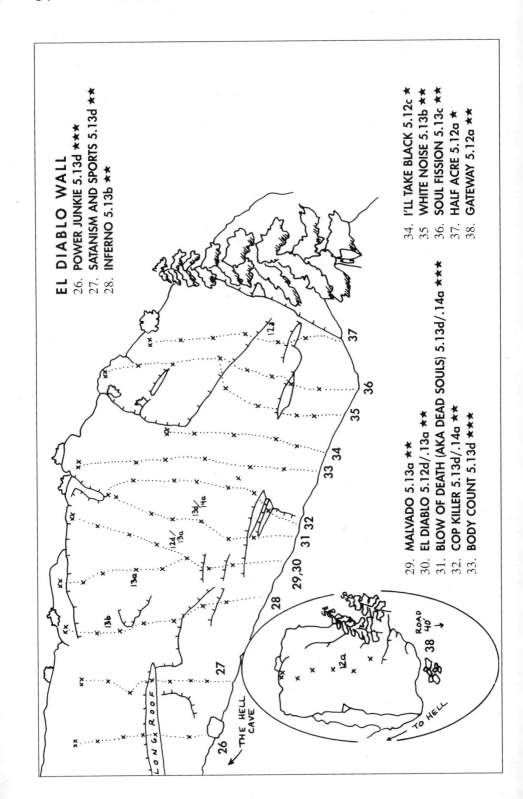

**EL DIABLO WALL**

26. POWER JUNKIE 5.13d ★★★
27. SATANISM AND SPORTS 5.13d ★★
28. INFERNO 5.13b ★★

29. MALVADO 5.13a ★★
30. EL DIABLO 5.12d/.13a ★★
31. BLOW OF DEATH (AKA DEAD SOULS) 5.13d/.14a ★★★
32. COP KILLER 5.13d/.14a ★★
33. BODY COUNT 5.13d ★★★

34. I'LL TAKE BLACK 5.12c ★
35. WHITE NOISE 5.13b ★★
36. SOUL FISSION 5.13c ★★
37. HALF ACRE 5.12a ★
38. GATEWAY 5.12a ★★

## EL DIABLO WALL

This wall is the eastern continuation of the **Hell Cave**.

26. **POWER JUNKIE 5.13d ★★★** "Power is the ultimate aphrodisiac." -Henry Kissinger. Fifteen moves of crimpy power endurance. Every move feels hard.
FA: Boone Speed.

27. **SATANISM AND SPORTS 5.13d ★★** (Project) Stay tuned. This promises to be stellar.
FA: Tim Wagner.

28. **INFERNO 5.13b ★★** Burn, baby, burn. Highly creative climbing.
FA: Dave Robinson.

29. **MALVADO 5.13a ★★** El Diablo's more sinister twin.
FA: Scott Frye.

30. **EL DIABLO 5.12d/.13a ★★** Powerful underclings and small edges. Well traveled.
FA: Txavo Vales.

31. **BLOW OF DEATH (AKA DEAD SOULS) 5.13d/.14a ★★★** "I do not believe that any man fears to be dead, but only the stroke of death." - Francis Bacon. A wicked fusion of dead points and small crimpy edges.
FA: Scott Franklin.

32. **COP KILLER 5.13d/.14a ★★** Difficult climbing to one fatal move. Perhaps the hardest crux move in the canyon.
FA: Geoff Weigand.

33. **BODY COUNT 5.13d ★★★** Longer than it looks—while working on it, the moves might feel fine, but on redpoint...
FA: Geoff Weigand.

34. **I'LL TAKE BLACK 5.12c ★** "Black as hell, strong as death, sweet as love." -Turkish proverb. A jamboree of small edges and big pulls.
FA: Boone Speed.

35. **WHITE NOISE 5.13b ★★** Technical, powerful climbing without a single crux move. Stick clip the second bolt.
FA: Mike Call.

36. **SOUL FISSION 5.13c ★★** A crimping nightmare. Attempted often, completed rarely.
FA: Boone Speed.

37. **HALF ACRE 5.12a ★** There are many acres of slopers on this bulging plot.
FA: Boone Speed.

38. **GATEWAY 5.12a ★★** Are you ready for the nether world? The first route encountered on the approach, this puzzler faces south, about fifty feet from the road. One bouldery sequence.
FA: Jeff Pedersen.

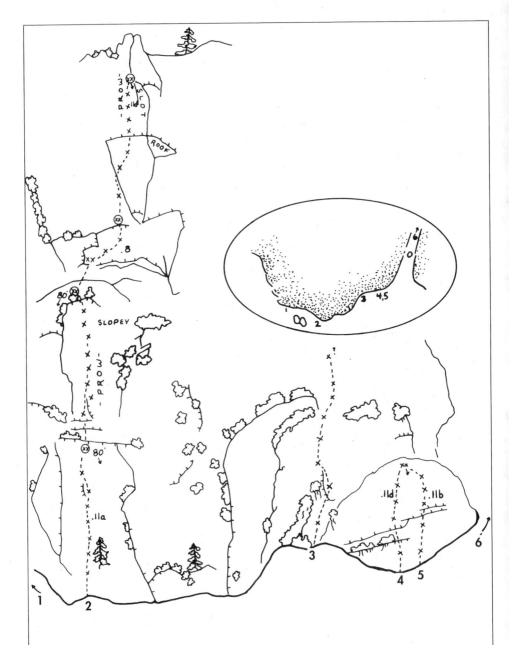

# B-52 WALL

1. SUPERINTENDENT'S LIMP DICKS 5.11c ★
2. SUSPECT 5.11d ★★
3. DESIRE (PROJECT).
4. SPATIAL UNREST 5.11d ★

5. ON WINGS OF BEAGLES 5.11b ★
6. ECTOPIC DISTRESS 5.11d

## B-52 WALL

North facing and shaded by trees, this is an ideal summer wall. Sloping holds are the allure of these routes, which require more than just brute force.

APPROACH: During low water it is possible to park at the upper end of the **Hell** parking area ( .65 miles up canyon from the TCNM flagpole) and follow a trail down to the stream. Cross the stream and head straight through the woods to reach the wall. During peak water flows, park .85 miles up canyon from the TCNM flagpole. (This is the first pullout on the right up canyon from the **Hell** parking.) Follow a trail downhill to a pipe bridge that crosses the stream, cross the stream and walk down canyon several hundred feet until the wall appears on the left. A quick hop through the trees reaches the base of the cliff. See Aerial View page 14.

1. **SUPERINTENDENT'S LIMP DICKS 5.11c** ★ A flaccid route, with one stiff sequence. Bouldery. It is located at the far left end of the wall. Not on topo.
   FA: Bill Boyle.

2. **SUSPECT 5.11d** ★★ Four pitches. The second is superb with a scary third clip and the final pitch has a reachy crux and ranks as one of the best in the canyon. One 55m rope works for the descent. Get above the trees and climb this route! The exact bolt count on topo is likely in error.
   FA: Bill Boyle.

3. **DESIRE (PROJECT)** Multi-pitch project.

4. **SPATIAL UNREST 5.11d** ★ Sloping holds on compact rock.
   FA: Bill Boyle.

5. **ON WINGS OF BEAGLES 5.11b** ★ The right and more reasonable line.
   FA: Bill Boyle.

6. **ECTOPIC DISTRESS 5.11d** Hike up the gully to the right of routes 4 and 5, crawl through a tube (the fallopian tube) to gain an upper tier. Continue up this gully until the route appears on the right. Expect some suspect rock.
   FA: Bill Boyle.

BAD BETA WALL
1. PROJECT
2. BAD BETA 5.11a ★

## BAD BETA WALL

A lonely wall with one route, good rock, shade, and serenity. Like many other canyon walls with this same northern aspect, expect more technical climbing.

APPROACH: During low water, park 1 mile up canyon from the TCNM flagpole at a pullout on the right (south) side of the road. Walk down the road 200' and hop across the stream. Walk up and right, following the base of the wall. During high-water times, park .85 miles up canyon from the TCNM flagpole at a pullout on the right (south) side of the road. Walk down a trail to a pipe bridge that crosses the stream. Cross the bridge, turn left and head up canyon, paralleling the stream. Several dicey sections are encountered when brush forces the path of least resistance down to the edge of the water. This can be avoided by thrashing up the embankment into the pines above. Continue heading up canyon until a cliff band is reached. Turn right and follow the base of the wall to its head. See Aerial View page 14.

1. **PROJECT** Two bolts(thus far) and a chain anchor.
2. **BAD BETA 5.11a** ★ Nine bolts of good climbing on slopers and edges.
   FA: Mark Allman.

## PINE TREE BUTTRESS

The two completed routes face west, which make for nice afternoon climbing on cool days. Several other projects in the area, when done, will beef up the route selection here. See Aerial View on page 14.

APPROACH: Park .95 miles up canyon from the TCNM flagpole on the left (north) side of the road. Walk up the road 150 feet to a trail that leads north past **Desperate But Not Serious** to a ledge, then turns west and heads to **Autonomy**. Three to five minutes.

1. **PUMP UP THE VOLUME** Project in the corner.

2. **AUTONOMY 5.11b ★**...this is what makes climbing special. A good route that looks "techweenie," but is actually quite a pump.
   FA: Bill Boyle.

3. **PROJECT** Around the corner to the right from **Autonomy**. South-facing.

4. **DESPERATE BUT NOT SERIOUS 5.11d ★** The black tower below and east of **Autonomy**. This has been described as a "mountaineering" type of route.
   FA: Lynn Ross and Conrad Anker.

5. **PROJECT** Around the corner 15 ft. to the right of **Desperate But Not Serious**. South-facing.

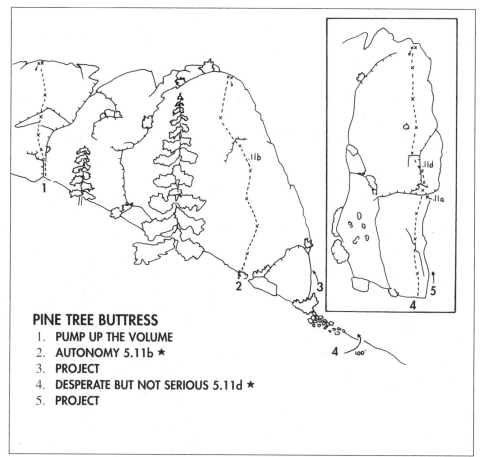

### PINE TREE BUTTRESS
1. PUMP UP THE VOLUME
2. AUTONOMY 5.11b ★
3. PROJECT
4. DESPERATE BUT NOT SERIOUS 5.11d ★
5. PROJECT

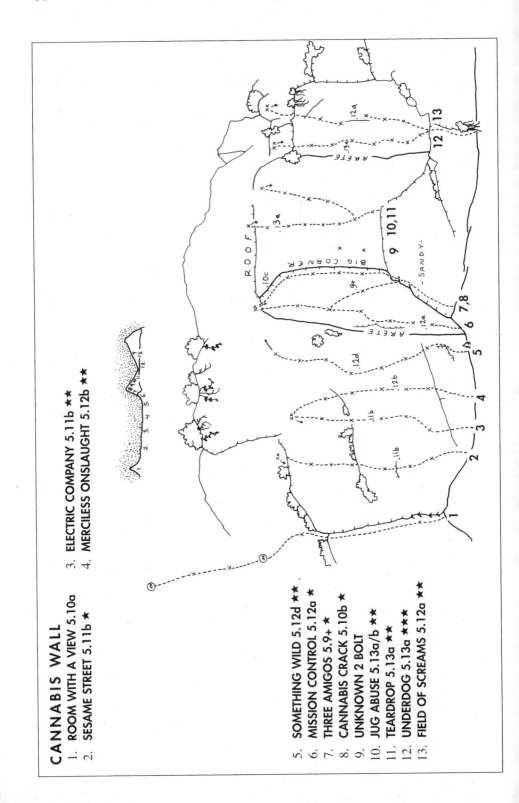

## CANNABIS WALL

1. ROOM WITH A VIEW 5.10a ★
2. SESAME STREET 5.11b ★

3. ELECTRIC COMPANY 5.11b ★★
4. MERCILESS ONSLAUGHT 5.12b ★★

5. SOMETHING WILD 5.12d ★★
6. MISSION CONTROL 5.12a ★
7. THREE AMIGOS 5.9+ ★
8. CANNABIS CRACK 5.10b ★
9. UNKNOWN 2 BOLT
10. JUG ABUSE 5.13a/b ★★
11. TEARDROP 5.13a ★★
12. UNDERDOG 5.13a ★★★
13. FIELD OF SCREAMS 5.12a ★★

## CANNABIS WALL

Shady and cool, the **Cannabis Wall** supplies an array of climbs ranging from the moderate in difficulty to the desperate. The routes here are characterized by powerful yet technical climbing. With few pockets, tenuous holds abound. See Aerial View page 14.

APPROACH: Park 1.0 miles up canyon from the TCNM flagpole on the right. Walk down canyon 200 ft., cross the stream, and the cliff will be staring you in the face. A high-water approach is possible, but more involved. Park .85 miles up canyon from the TCNM flagpole at a pullout. Walk down a trail to a pipe bridge that crosses the stream. Cross the bridge, turn left and head up canyon, paralleling the stream. Several dicey sections are encountered when brush forces the path of least resistance down to the edge of the water. This can be avoided by thrashing up an embankment and into the pine trees above. Continue heading up canyon, until a cliff band is reached which requires a careful traverse on a ledge system over the stream, ending, finally, at the **Cannabis Wall.**

1. **ROOM WITH A VIEW 5.10a** Two pitches. Start in an open book with a bolt on the left side of the wall. Exact bolt count unknown.
   FA: Carl Horton.

2. **SESAME STREET 5.11b ★** You too may become like Oscar the Grouch on this tribute to slopers. Harder than the name suggests. The cruxes are bouldery.
   FA: Bill Boyle.

3. **ELECTRIC COMPANY 5.11b ★★** Shockingly good. The crux is inobvious.
   FA: Boone Speed and Bill Boyle.

4. **MERCILESS ONSLAUGHT 5.12b ★★** Merciless for the maladroit; just plain hard.
   FA: Mike Beck and Vince Adams.

5. **SOMETHING WILD 5.12d ★★** Beguiling moves up nothingness. Dicey.
   FA: Boone Speed.

6. **MISSION CONTROL 5.12a ★** NASA climbing. (Never Assume you'll Send it Automatically.) Launch into the bouldering moves at the start which mark the crux.
   FA: Vince Adams.

7. **THREE AMIGOS 5.9+ ★** Starts in the corner and crosses the face to join **Mission Control**.
   FA: Jeff Pedersen, Boone Speed and Vince Adams.

8. **CANNABIS CRACK 5.10b ★** Kind of sporty. Put in on lead with gear.
   FA: Vince Adams.

9. **UNKNOWN 2 BOLT**

10. **JUG ABUSE 5.13a/b ★★** Sophisticated power moves lead to an abusing finish.
    FA: Jeff Pedersen.

11. **TEARDROP 5.13a ★★** "I wept not, so to stone within I grew." -Dante Alighieri. Exit right off **Jug Abuse.**
    FA: Hidataka Suzuki.

12. **UNDERDOG 5.13a ★★★** A tweak-fest up the right side of the arête.
    FA: Boone Speed.

13. **FIELD OF SCREAMS 5.12a ★★** This route actually has a couple finger locks. Good, steep climbing with a fourth clip that is hard. After the first ascent of this route, Bill Boyle leaned back at the chains to get lowered and noticed his harness buckle completely undone and held in place with only the velcro—what a scream!
    FA: Jeff Pedersen and Bill Boyle.

## MEMBRANE AND ISOLATION AREA

One of the most popular walls in American Fork Canyon, **The Membrane** has almost instant access, and steep climbing on edges and killer pockets. The northern exposure makes **The Membrane** cool even on the hottest summer days. In the spring, however, the pockets can sometimes be wet. See Aerial View page 14.

APPROACH: Park 1.0 miles up canyon from the TCNM flagpole at a large pullout. At the upper end of the parking area, a trail leads down to the stream. Cross the stream (along a scary pole, early '95) and you are at **The Membrane.** To reach the **Isolation Area,** walk along the base of **The Membrane** and continue east (up canyon) through the trees for one minute. **Isolation** is tucked inside of a pleasant alcove. No options exist for a high water approach other than crossing the dam up stream several hundred feet. However, this is strictly illegal.

## ISOLATION WALL

Cool and quiet, these routes pack a punch.

1. **SIBERIA 5.12c/d** ★ Desolate climbing up the left side of the wall.
   FA: Mike Beck.
2. **ISOLATION 5.12b/c** ★★ Powerful variety on bullet proof rock. The arms fade fast on this unrelenting route.
   FA: Boone Speed and Jeff Pedersen.
3. **WILDERNESS 5.12a/b** ★ Boulder moves on wicked small holds.
   FA: Jeff Pedersen.

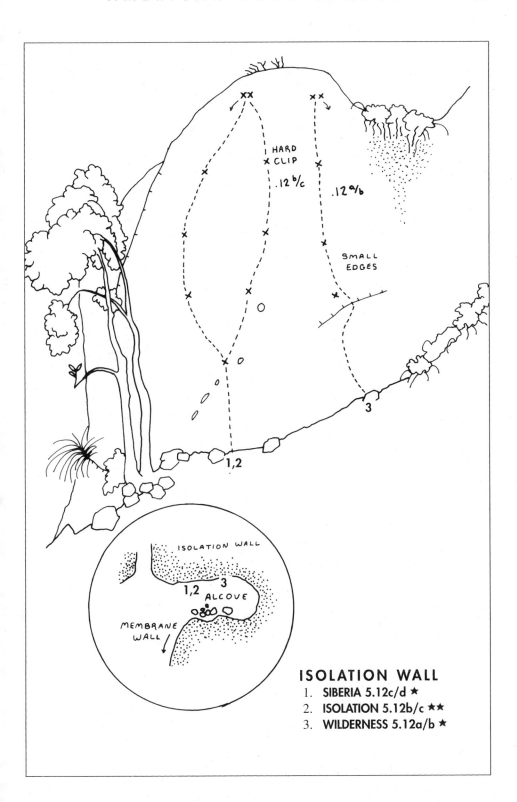

HARD CLIP

.12 b/c

.12 a/b

SMALL EDGES

3

1,2

ISOLATION WALL

1,2   3
      ALCOVE

MEMBRANE WALL

## ISOLATION WALL
1. SIBERIA 5.12c/d ★
2. ISOLATION 5.12b/c ★★
3. WILDERNESS 5.12a/b ★

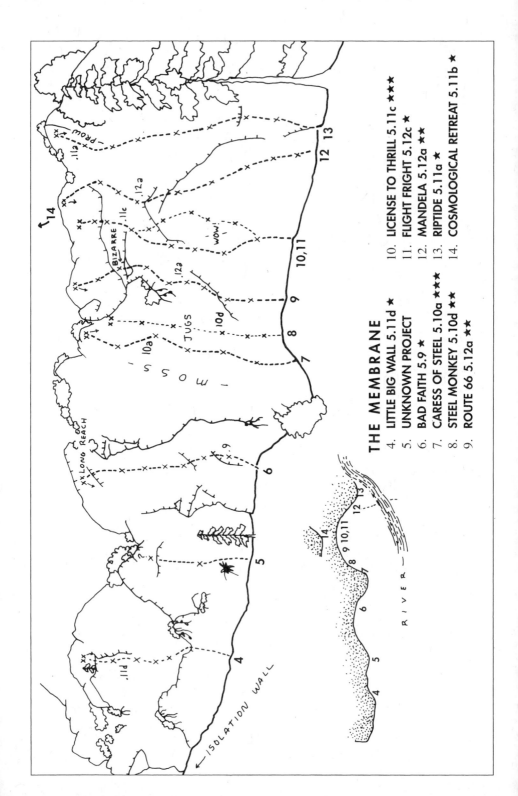

## THE MEMBRANE

4. LITTLE BIG WALL 5.11d ★
5. UNKNOWN PROJECT
6. BAD FAITH 5.9
7. CARESS OF STEEL 5.10a ★★★
8. STEEL MONKEY 5.10d ★★
9. ROUTE 66 5.12a ★★

10. LICENSE TO THRILL 5.11c ★★★
11. FLIGHT FRIGHT 5.12c ★
12. MANDELA 5.12a ★★
13. RIPTIDE 5.11a ★
14. COSMOLOGICAL RETREAT 5.11b ★

## THE MEMBRANE

Though frequently crowded, these routes are some of the canyon's finest.

4. **LITTLE BIG WALL 5.11d** ★ Short, with a devious bulge. Better than it looks.
   FA: Pete Takeda, 1989.

5. **UNKNOWN PROJECT**

6. **BAD FAITH 5.9** ★ "It was the schoolboy who said, `Faith is believing what you know ain't so'." -Mark Twain. A good route for the fun-loving.
   FA: Bill Boyle.

7. **CARESS OF STEEL 5.10a** ★★★ A classic jug haul that should not be missed.
   FA: Scott Unice and Bill Boyle.

8. **STEEL MONKEY 5.10d** ★★ Big pockets and one big reach.

9. **ROUTE 66 5.12a** ★★ You'll get your kicks with finger buckets and flabbergasting roofs. The upper roof can take a long time to figure out.
   FA: Bill Boyle.

10. **LICENSE TO THRILL 5.11c** ★★★ One of American Fork's best. Pockets, a roof, pumper. Do it!
    FA: Vince Adams.

11. **FLIGHT FRIGHT 5.12c** ★ Take the non-stop line between **License to Thrill** and **Mandela.** Finish on **License to Thrill**.
    FA: Vince Adams.

12. **MANDELA 5.12a** ★★ Persevere through stems and sloper holds.
    FA: Bill Boyle

13. **RIPTIDE 5.11a** ★ Steep climbing to an exciting final prow. Popular.
    FA: Bill Boyle.

14. **COSMOLOGICAL RETREAT 5.11b** ★ The cosmic is largely comic. Very few climbers have journeyed up to this route. It has an unforgiving mantle at the top. No topo.
    FA: Bill Boyle.


Overheard at the crags:
"The drop-knee is the mantle of the '90's."

# MANY AMERICAN FORK GEMS STARTED OUT THIS WAY

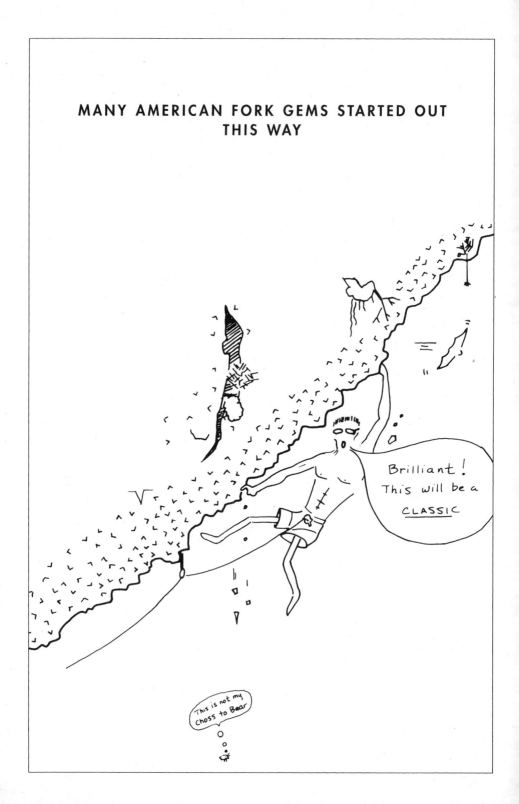

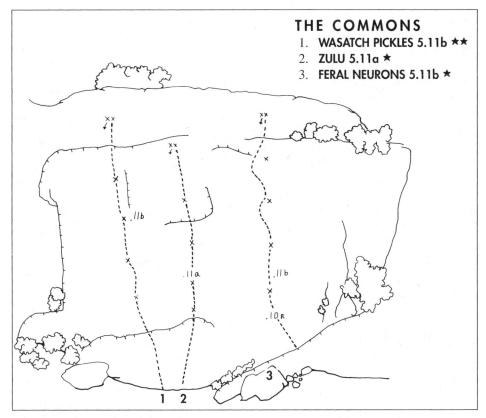

**THE COMMONS**
1. WASATCH PICKLES 5.11b ★★
2. ZULU 5.11a ★
3. FERAL NEURONS 5.11b ★

## THE COMMONS

**The Commons** is a cool, shady area with three routes on a black dolomite slab. The rock is excellent and reclines at an angle between 85 and 90 degrees. See Aerial View page 14.

APPROACH: Park at Hanging Rock picnic grounds 1.15 miles up canyon from the TCNM flagpole. Cross the stream on the west side of the picnic area and scramble up the dirt and talus, staying close to the base of the main wall. **The Commons** resides at the head of the steep slope (about ten minutes). When exploring the rock to the west of **The Commons** be extremely careful. Any rocks that roll down the slope will be death missiles to climbers on **The Membrane** and **Isolation Walls**.

1. **WASATCH PICKLES 5.11b ★★** A technical route that is "out of character" for American Fork.
   FA: Scott Unice.

2. **ZULU 5.11a ★** One stumping sequence at the bottom.
   FA: Bill Boyle.

3. **FERAL NEURONS 5.11b ★** "Each of us, a cell of awareness, imperfect and incomplete." -Neil Peart. It takes real savvy to succeed at the overhanging start. The first clip is a scare.
   FA: Bill Boyle.

Jeff Pedersen leading the **Blue Mask [5.13c] The Billboard**

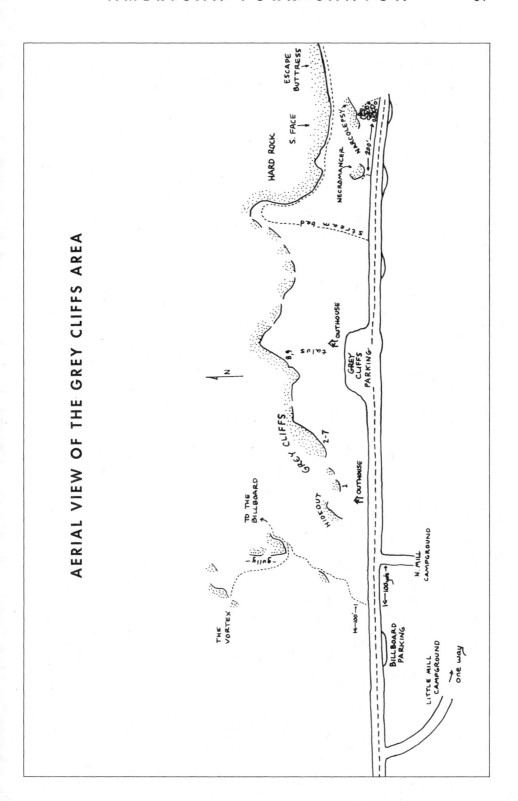

AERIAL VIEW OF THE GREY CLIFFS AREA

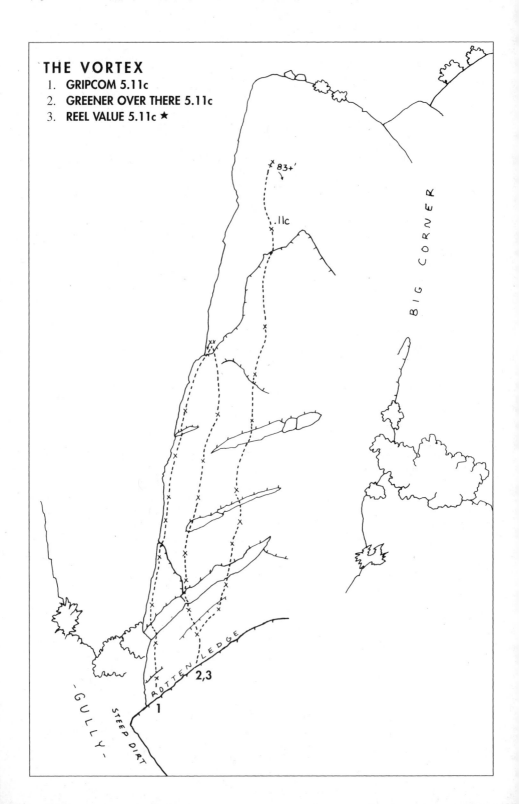

**THE VORTEX**
1. GRIPCOM 5.11c
2. GREENER OVER THERE 5.11c
3. REEL VALUE 5.11c ★

83+'

.11c

BIG CORNER

ROTTEN LEDGE

2,3

1

GULLY

STEEP DIRT

## THE VORTEX

Unlike its namesake, this **Vortex** is not drawing many people towards it. However, three routes exist here, and the rock is cleaning up. The routes have cool moves and good positions.

APPROACH: Park 1.5 miles up canyon from the TCNM flagpole at a small pullout on the right (south) side of the road, (.2 miles up canyon from the entrance to Little Mill Campground). There is limited parking here, so continue up to the next pullout if the lower lot is full. From the lower area, cross the road and walk 100 feet up canyon to a small cairn at the base of an east diagonaling trail. (This is the trail to **The Billboard**.) After a short distance the trail contours along the base of a rock outcrop and a bit higher you come to a smooth, Verdon-like wall. At the bottom left side of this wall, head west into a gully. Scramble up the gully for 150 feet and look for bolts on an east-facing prow on the west side of the gully. Approximately 15 minutes. See Aerial View page 69.

1. **GRIPCOM 5.11c** Not the best rock quality, but fun nonetheless.
   FA: Bill Boyle.
2. **GREENER OVER THERE 5.11c** It is definitely greener elsewhere.
   FA: Bill Boyle.
3. **REEL VALUE 5.11c** ★ "Nowadays people know the price of everything and the value of nothing." -Oscar Wilde. A long and continuous lead, with scary rock and cool moves.
   FA: Bill Boyle.

Steve Carruthers pumping **Gridlock [5.12a/b] The Billboard**

## THE BILLBOARD

With spectacular views of North Timpanogos and loads of hard climbs, **The Billboard** is possibly the finest crag in American Fork. It faces south and sits high on the north side of the canyon, creating an ideal winter training ground. However, it is also comfortable in mid-summer before noon on **The Gridwall** as it is all day long in **The Shining Cave.** **The Gridwall** tips to 100 degrees and has bolt spacing a bit more sporty than other areas in the canyon. **The Shining Cave** and **Apetizer Wall** offer much steeper climbing. During the first year of activity at **The Billboard,** a crude topo of the climbs was drawn on a large piece of canvas and stashed in **The Shining Cave.** Faded and torn, it remains in the archive today, its hidden treasures waiting to be unrolled.

APPROACH: Park 1.5 miles up canyon from the TCNM flagpole at a small pullout on the right (south) side of the road. (.2 miles up canyon from the entrance to Little Mill Campground). There is limited parking here, so continue up to the next pullout if the lower lot is full. From the lower area, cross the road and walk 100 feet up canyon to a small cairn at the base of an east diagonaling trail. The trail leads steeply up to the cliff from here. This hike takes about 30-40 minutes and is virtually impossible to describe, so stay on the trail. One comment: the trail tends to always go up and RIGHT. See Aerial View page 69.

1.  **RUNAWAY TRAIN 5.12b/c** ★ Located roughly one third of the way up **The Billboard** trail. The trail passes along the base of a smooth, Verdon-like wall. **Runaway Train** is 100 feet higher, to the left of a prominent cave. Climb up the overhanging prow on strenuous holds.
    FA: Jim Howe.

2.  **CLUB A 5.12a** ★ Located roughly two thirds of the way up **The Billboard** trail. The trail passes right along the base of this east-facing wall. Brutal climbing on small edges and sidepulls. Only climbers of the very exclusive club will flash this route.
    FA: Doug Heinrich

Routes 3-6 are found on the slightly overhanging **Apetizer Wall**.

3.  **GORILLAS IN THE SNOW 5.12b** ★★ After dealing with a slopey, bouldery crux at the roof, the terrain above will feel like hiking.
    FA: Bill Boyle and Boone Speed.

4.  **APETIZER 5.12** ★★★ Excellent. A package deal up the center of the face. This ought to whet the appetite.
    FA: Bill Boyle and Boone Speed.

5.  **MONKEY BRAINS 5.13a** ★★★ A techno-powerful line with small edges. Rumored to have one of the single hardest moves in the canyon.
    FA: Boone Speed.

6.  **PROJECT** Once known as **Limestone Cowboy,** the future of this project remains uncertain.

Routes 7-20 are located in or on the flanks of the huge **Shining Cave.**

7.  **FANG 5.11c** A wild route that starts with mountaineering and finishes with 20 feet of sharp crack climbing.
    FA: Bill Boyle.

8.  **THE ONE 5.12a** ★ The unique crab-climbing under the roof is awkward, but fun in a strange sort of way. Cross to the right beneath the roof to a bolt, then climb straight up to a two-bolt anchor.
    FA: Bill Boyle.

9.  **THE ONE THAT GOT AWAY 5.12b/c** ★★ Climb **The One** to its anchors, then take a tour up the steep wall above. Reachy, with hard moves, and a pump to the chains.
    FA: Bill Boyle.

10. **EATING THE GUN 5.12d** ★★ A real choker—a true fight to the finish. Excellent.
    FA: Bill Boyle.

11. **REDRUM 5.13b** ★★★ The fist jams shouldn't discourage— it is a great route.
    FA: Jeff Pedersen and Merrill Bitter.

12. **BLUE MASK 5.13c** ★★★ Talk about wild. Upside-down more than vertical, this one takes the cake. A paragon.
    FA: Jeff Pedersen.

13. **INVISIBLE MAN 5.13b/c** ★★★ Who? More wildness that begins on **Blue Mask,** but heads straight up at the eighth bolt and then left again across imperceptible features. Luckily, you can work out the crux moves from the big pine tree.
    FA: Jeff Pedersen.

14. **ATMOSPHERE 5.13a** ★★★ "Space flights are merely an escape, a fleeing away from oneself, because it is easier to go to Mars or to the moon than it is to penetrate one's own being." -Carl Jung. Difficult climbing starts on the **Blue Mask** and continues straight up at the eighth bolt.
    FA: Jeff Pedersen.

15. **THE SHINING 5.13c** ★★★ One of the canyon's finest. A low percentage crux awaits at the lip.
    FA: Boone Speed.

16. **THIS MUST BE THE PICKLE 5.12d/.13a** ★★ A powerful line with roofs, pockets and several wild sequences. The bonus question: what does the name mean?
    FA: Bill Boyle.

17. **AMBUSH 5.12a/b** ★★ Watch out for the hidden, awaiting crux. Cross **The Whining** and continue up and right. This route actually has a good slab finish.
    FA: Bill Boyle.

18. **THE WHINING 5.12a** ★ With good rock and good moves this is destined to become more popular. Follows the left arching crack and corner system.
    FA: Bill Boyle.

19. **PROJECT** A three bolt line to the right of **The Whining.** Conceived as a variation that leads to the anchors on **Ambush.**

20. **DWARF TOSS 5.12c** ★★ Just a guess: a reachy move might be in order? A hard crank to a hidden pocket is the crux, but the slab above shouldn't be taken lightly.
    FA: Doug Heinrich.

Routes 21-30 are on what is collectively known as **The Gridwall**.

21. **INVITATION TO THE BLUES 5.11d ★★** People have been known to ride into the blue while staring at the chains. The roofs are good.
FA: Bill Boyle.

22. **SMALL CHANGE 5.11a ★** A good warm-up route with stems, layaways and baffling moves.
FA: Bill Boyle.

23. **ERECTION OR EJECTION 5.11d ★★** Get it up for these pockets of pleasure.
FA: Bill Boyle.

24. **MUSIC FOR CHAMELEONS 5.11d ★★** Great pockets. Save some juice for the last clip.
FA: Bill Boyle.

25. **DEATH OF A SAILSMAN 5.12a ★★** "A salesman has got to dream, boy. It comes with the territory." -Arthur Miller. A plumb line up the center of the wall.
FA: Bill Boyle and Boone Speed.

26. **GRIDLOCK 5.12a ★★** or **5.12b/c ★★** The final route done on **The Gridwall**. Climb a tree to reach the second bolt and then step across, or climb the direct start (5.12b/c). You can traverse left to **Death of a Sailsman's** anchors to get off with one 50m rope.
FA: Boone Speed, Jeff Pedersen and Bill Boyle.

27. **AMERICAN FLYERS 5.12a ★★** or **5.12b/c ★★** Many climbers have gained some frequent flyer miles on this jaunt. Climb a tree to reach the second bolt and the step across, or climb the direct start (5.12b/c). Remember to take the right fork.
FA: Jeff Pedersen.

28. **TO HELL ON A ROCKET 5.12b ★★** or **5.12c/d ★★** The cruxes seem to be just before clipping the bolts. Stick clip the second bolt and climb the tree at the base of **American Flyers** to reach the starting holds, or climb the direct start (5.12c/d).
FA: Jeff Pedersen.

29. **BEELINE 5.12b ★★★** Pocket perfection.
FA: Boone Speed.

30. **THE ANARCHIST 5.11c/d ★** There is no law and order to nature's destruction. Once an easier route (see below), part of which has since fallen off, it has been resurrected and the remaining pockets now lead up more formidable terrain.
FA: Darren Knezek.

The far right side of **The Billboard Wall,** including a route called **Operation Mindcrime**, fell off during the spring of 1991. Several car sized blocks rolled down to the road. The destruction was amazing—huge trees broken like twigs, rocks pulverized, and a wide scar that ran from **The Billboard** down to the canyon bottom. For several seasons, a fresh boulder several hundred feet down **The Billboard** approach trail still had a bolt and hanger in place. The hanger is gone now, but the bolt remains as a testament to the powerful forces of nature.

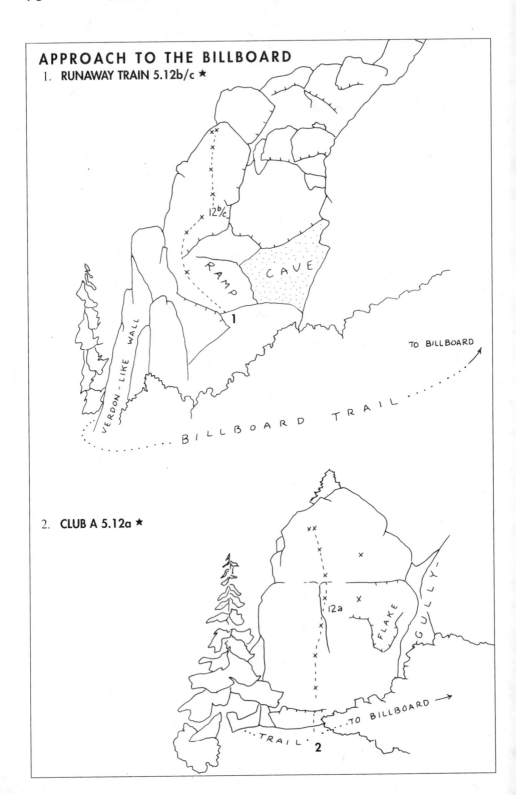

APPROACH TO THE BILLBOARD
1. RUNAWAY TRAIN 5.12b/c ★

2. CLUB A 5.12a ★

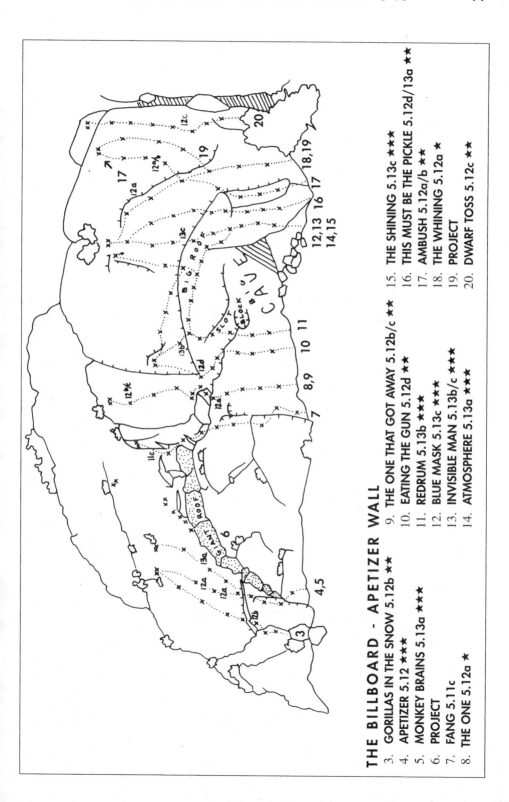

## THE BILLBOARD - APETIZER WALL

3. GORILLAS IN THE SNOW 5.12b ★★
4. APETIZER 5.12 ★★
5. MONKEY BRAINS 5.13a ★★★
6. PROJECT
7. FANG 5.11c
8. THE ONE 5.12a ★

9. THE ONE THAT GOT AWAY 5.12b/c ★★
10. EATING THE GUN 5.12d ★★
11. REDRUM 5.13b ★★★
12. BLUE MASK 5.13c ★★★
13. INVISIBLE MAN 5.13b/c ★★★
14. ATMOSPHERE 5.13a ★★★

15. THE SHINING 5.13c ★★★
16. THIS MUST BE THE PICKLE 5.12d/13a ★★
17. AMBUSH 5.12a/b ★★
18. THE WHINING 5.12a ★
19. PROJECT
20. DWARF TOSS 5.12c ★★

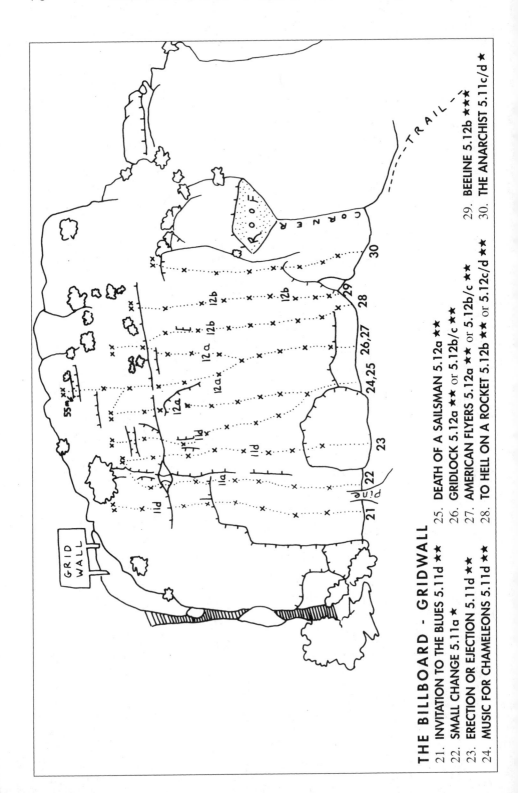

# THE BILLBOARD - GRIDWALL

21. INVITATION TO THE BLUES 5.11d ★★
22. SMALL CHANGE 5.11a ★
23. ERECTION OR EJECTION 5.11d ★★
24. MUSIC FOR CHAMELEONS 5.11d ★★
25. DEATH OF A SAILSMAN 5.12a ★★
26. GRIDLOCK 5.12a ★★ or 5.12b/c ★★
27. AMERICAN FLYERS 5.12a ★★ or 5.12b/c ★★
28. TO HELL ON A ROCKET 5.12b ★★ or 5.12c/d ★★
29. BEELINE 5.12b ★★
30. THE ANARCHIST 5.11c/d ★

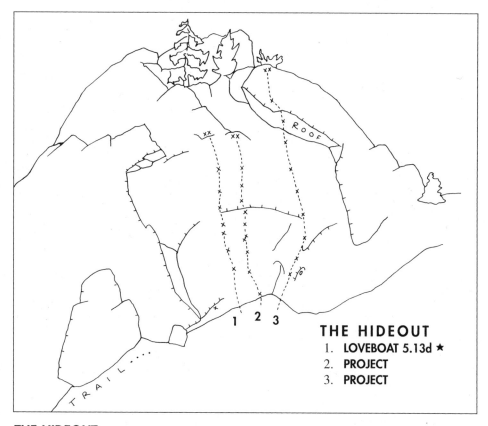

**THE HIDEOUT**
1. **LOVEBOAT 5.13d** ★
2. **PROJECT**
3. **PROJECT**

## THE HIDEOUT

This mini-cave, hidden behind a grove of oak trees, conceals one of the canyon's hardest routes. It is steep here, and when the other projects are redpointed, this wall will yield a number of wrenching test pieces.

APPROACH: Park 1.7 miles up canyon from the TCNM flagpole at **The Grey Cliffs** Picnic Area. This is .4 miles up canyon from the entrance to Little Mill Campground. Park here only if it is not too full; otherwise pull off the road at the pulloffs a bit further up canyon to leave room for the picnickers to park. Walk 200 feet down canyon from the main **Grey Cliffs** parking area to an outhouse on the right (north) side of the road. Between the outhouse and the picnic table just down canyon, follow a trail up the slope. The key is to head left each time brush impedes the way straight up. Eventually you will reach the wall on the left which is followed up to **The Hideout**. About five minutes. See Aerial View page 69.

1. **LOVEBOAT 5.13d** ★ A brutal cruise out the left side of the cave. Bring your forearms for this power endurance problem. A jug broke off on an early ascent, but the route has since been redpointed.
   FA: Geoff Weigand.
2. **PROJECT** The middle line.
3. **PROJECT** The journey on the right.

## THE GREY CLIFFS
1.  THE PREMISE 5.11c/d ★
2.  SNAKED FROM NEW YORK 5.13b ★
3.  FORTY SOMETHING 5.12d ★★
4.  SYLLOGISM 5.12c/d ★★★
5.  TOO YOUNG TO BE HUMAN 5.12a/b ★★★
6.  SLIMABEING 5.11c ★
7.  THE ARGUMENT 5.12a ★

## THE GREY CLIFFS

There are actually three distinct walls here. Each has its own characteristics but all offer fine climbing on very steep rock. Mostly east facing, these walls are perfect on cool mornings or warm afternoons.

APPROACH: Park at **The Grey Cliffs** Picnic Area 1.7 miles up canyon from the TCNM flagpole. This is .4 miles up canyon from the entrance to Little Mill Campground. If the lot is too full, use one of the pullouts further up canyon and leave the picnickers room to park. The approaches are short, and are described at the beginning of each wall. See Aerial View page 69.

From the main parking area, walk down canyon 150 feet, turn right (north) and walk through the trees to this small, radically steep wall.

1.  **THE PREMISE 5.11c/d** ★ This route emerges from the trees, turns several bulges, and concludes with a desperate exit.
    FA: Bill Boyle.

Routes 2-7 are located above and left of the main parking at **The Grey Cliffs** picnic area. They are easily seen from the parking lot. Walk through the trees towards the cliff, catch a trail up to the base of the wall, and traverse left along an exposed ledge to the base of the routes. Three minutes.

2.  **SNAKED FROM NEW YORK 5.13b** ★ Wicked hard climbing on the far left side of the wall.

3.  **FORTY SOMETHING 5.12d** ★★ "At twenty years of age, the will reigns; at thirty, the wit; at forty, the judgment." -Henry Grattan. Climbing that attacks the aesthetic wall via some bouldery cruxes. Strenuous pulls.
    FA: Bill Boyle.

4.  **SYLLOGISM 5.12c/d** ★★★ Prove yourself on this "da kind jug haul."
    FA: Boone Speed.

5.  **TOO YOUNG TO BE HUMAN 5.12a/b** ★★★ Start on **Slimabeing** and split off left. The unfledged climber will likely fail on the overhanging and very strenuous pocket moves. Quality.
    FA: Bill Boyle.

6.  **SLIMABEING 5.11c** ★ A good route with 10 feet of handjamming near the top. Big air.
    FA: Bill Boyle.

7.  **THE ARGUMENT 5.12a** ★ The right route on the cliff. Reachy moves over roofs with several rests in between.
    FA: Bill Boyle.

The next two routes are located up and right 200 feet from the main **Grey Cliff** wall. This southeast facing cliff is evident from the road. Approach by walking up the talus slope directly behind the outhouse at the main **Grey Cliffs** Parking Area.

8.  **PROJECT** looks good.
    FA: Bill Boyle.

9.  **ALL MEN ARE MORTAL 5.12a/b** ★★ "All men think all men mortal but themselves." -Edward Young. A whirlwind of sequences is needed to overcome all the obstacles of this route. Small edges.
    FA: Bill Boyle.

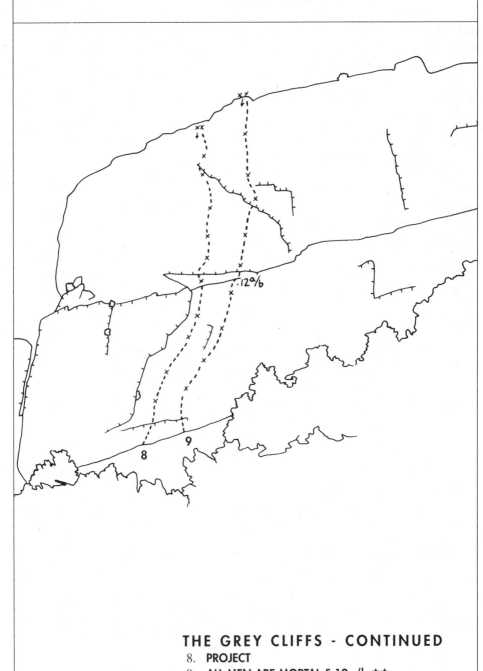

**THE GREY CLIFFS - CONTINUED**
8.  PROJECT
9.  ALL MEN ARE MORTAL 5.12a/b ★★

Doug Heinrich sending **Too Young to be Human [5.12a/b] Grey Cliffs**    Photo: Scott Markewitz

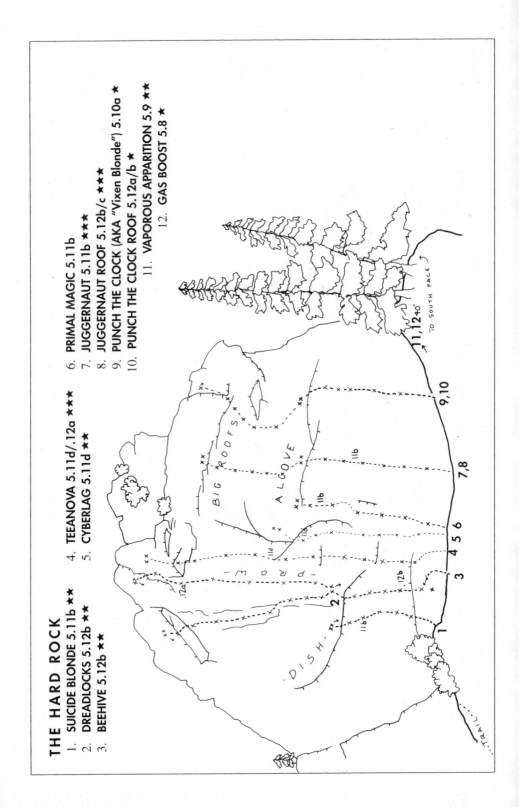

THE HARD ROCK

1. SUICIDE BLONDE 5.11b ★★
2. DREADLOCKS 5.12b ★★
3. BEEHIVE 5.12b ★★

4. TEEANOVA 5.11d/.12a ★★★
5. CYBERLAG 5.11d ★★

6. PRIMAL MAGIC 5.11b
7. JUGGERNAUT 5.11b ★★★
8. JUGGERNAUT ROOF 5.12b/c ★★★
9. PUNCH THE CLOCK (AKA "Vixen Blonde") 5.10a ★
10. PUNCH THE CLOCK ROOF 5.12a/b ★
11. VAPOROUS APPARITION 5.9 ★★
12. GAS BOOST 5.8 ★

## THE HARD ROCK

A banquet of pockets greets the visitor to **The Hard Rock** area. Composed of four separate walls, many of the canyon's most pocketed routes are here, and a wide range of difficulties are found. With climbs on both the west and south faces, **The Hard Rock** walls catch shade or sun, depending on the aspect, and **The Escape Buttress** can be sunny even during the winter.

APPROACH: Park at **The Grey Cliffs** Picnic Area 1.7 miles up canyon from the TCNM flagpole. This is also .4 miles up canyon from the entrance to Little Mill Campground. Park just up canyon at one of the other pullouts if the picnic area is almost full. Walk up the road 300 feet from the main **Grey Cliffs** Picnic Area to the first (most western) of two trails that lead to the left (north). Walk up a surprisingly good trail following a shallow drainage which leads up to the west facing part of the wall. The spring of 1993 wrought havoc to this entire area when a huge avalanche roared down, ripping up all the vegetation and burying the road for several months. See Aerial View page 69.

1. **SUICIDE BLONDE 5.11b** ★★ The left route on the lower wall begins with wrapper holds and ends with delicate climbing to reach a ledge.
   FA: Drew Bedford.

2. **DREADLOCKS 5.12b** ★★ The left route on the upper tier. Finger locks, a hand jam, and a really cool pocket move require a totally rasta attitude, mahn!
   FA: Drew Bedford.

3. **BEEHIVE 5.12b** ★★ Usually done in one pitch, but can be broken into two. The first section favors power (.12b), the second taxes the endurance (.12a). Stick clip the first bolt and be prepared for full meltdown.
   FA: Drew Bedford.

4. **TEEANOVA 5.11d/.12a** ★★★ Classic. A very steep jug haul that will leave you laughing at the good pockets, but gasping at your forearms. Three big overhangs, two big rests.
   FA: Brian Smoot.

5. **CYBERLAG 5.11d** ★★ Hidden pockets, a monodoigt move, a bulge; a laudable excursion. Hollow rock forced the chain anchor to be right of its ideal position.
   FA: Brian Smoot.

6. **PRIMAL MAGIC 5.11b** A hocus pocus crux—now you see a path through it, now you don't.
   FA: Brian Smoot.

7. **JUGGERNAUT 5.11b** ★★★ Clean, technical face climbing with some killer pockets. Outstanding.
   FA: Drew Bedford.

8. **JUGGERNAUT ROOF 5.12b/c** ★★★ Jug or not?
   FA: Drew Bedford.

9. **PUNCH THE CLOCK (AKA "VIXEN BLONDE") 5.10a** ★ "I am a friend of the working man, and I would rather be his friend than be one." -Clarence Darrow. Pockets, edges and steep stuff that ends in the alcove.
   FA: Drew Bedford.

10. **PUNCH THE CLOCK ROOF 5.12a/b** ★ Ninety percent pockets, ten percent blank rock. Gymnastic.
FA: Drew Bedford.

From **Punch the Clock** walk forty feet right (south) to find the next two routes on a short, south-facing wall.

11. **VAPOROUS APPARITION 5.9** ★★ This is the left route. Jugs and pockets with a balancy third clip. This route should clean up well. 5 bolts. Not on topo.
FA: Brian Smoot.

12. **GAS BOOST 5.8** ★ A juggy excursion that is steeper than it looks. 4 bolts. Not on topo.
FA: Brian Smoot.

## THE HARD ROCK SOUTH FACE

A haven for moderate routes that require balance and footwork as well as some big pockets to yard up on. Although not of the highest quality, the climbs here are fun and very well traveled. This wall catches sun until evening.

APPROACH: See the approach information in **The Hard Rock** section.

The following routes are located on the south face of **The Hard Rock** wall. From **Gas Boost** continue heading right (south) along the base of the wall. Round the corner and walk uphill through the brush to reach the base of the climbs.

1. **EIGHT TO ELEVEN 5.11b/c** ★ A moderate first pitch is followed by exposed pulling over the roofs. Both pitches can be combined to make one long pitch.
FA: Brian Smoot, Jonathon Smoot, and Brandon Prince.

2. **STOIC CALCULUS 5.8** ★★ A 5.8 climb for 5.10 leaders. Long runouts, but fun nonetheless. Popular.
FA: Scott Unice and Tim Egbert

3. **ROCKAPELLA 5.7** ★★ Immensely popular. Quality.
FA: Brian and Vickie Smoot.

4. **PLATINUM BLONDE 5.10a** ★ A long route that gobbles up all of a fifty-five meter rope. With a shorter rope, belay on the ledge at the first bolt. Continuous and sporty.
FA: Tim Egbert and Scott Unice.

5. **WINDS OF FIRE 5.10** One hundred feet to the east of **Platinum Blonde** is a long prow capped by a roof. **Winds of Fire** climbs this prow via a series of exposed pockets.
FA: Scott Unice

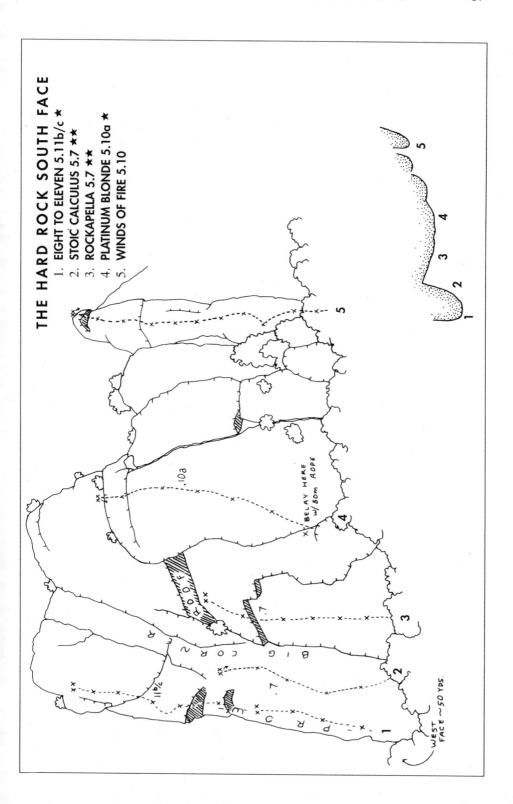

## THE HARD ROCK SOUTH FACE

1. EIGHT TO ELEVEN 5.11b/c ★
2. STOIC CALCULUS 5.7 ★★
3. ROCKAPELLA 5.7 ★★
4. PLATINUM BLONDE 5.10a ★
5. WINDS OF FIRE 5.10

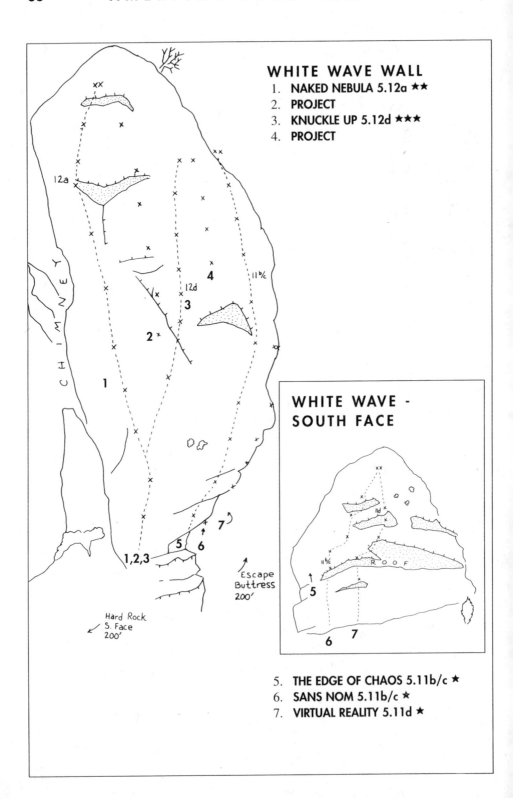

**WHITE WAVE WALL**
1. NAKED NEBULA 5.12a ★★
2. PROJECT
3. KNUCKLE UP 5.12d ★★★
4. PROJECT

**WHITE WAVE - SOUTH FACE**

5. THE EDGE OF CHAOS 5.11b/c ★
6. SANS NOM 5.11b/c ★
7. VIRTUAL REALITY 5.11d ★

## WHITE WAVE WALL

This pillar is riddled with pockets. Steep climbing is the game here, so expect big pumps on good holds. With west and south faces, the **White Wave Wall** is a perfect spring or fall cliff.

APPROACH: See the approach information in **The Hard Rock** section. From **The Hard Rock South Face** area, continue right (east) along a trail for 200 feet. The trail passes below the **White Wave Wall**.

1.  **NAKED NEBULA 5.12a** ★★ Expose yourself to this mass of prime climbing. Reaches between steep jugs and poor rests.
    FA: Brian Smoot.

2.  **PROJECT** Cut left after the third or fourth bolt on **Knuckle Up** and climb directly up the center of the face.

3.  **KNUCKLE UP 5.12d** ★★★ As good as it gets, up the steepest part of the wall. Deluxe two-finger pocket climbing with one big move.
    FA: Drew Bedford.

4.  **PROJECT** A more strenuous variation to **The Edge of Chaos.**

5.  **THE EDGE OF CHAOS 5.11b/c** ★ Follows the outer edge of the big arch and catches some big air. Pumpy. The better holds force you onto the steeper rock.
    FA: Brian Smoot.

6.  **SANS NOM 5.11b/c** ★ Steep and fun. Should clean up to become on par with the rest of the wall.

7.  **VIRTUAL REALITY 5.11d** ★ The bolt line on the far right is steep and juggy with classic pockets that should clean up nicely.
    FA: Brian Smoot.

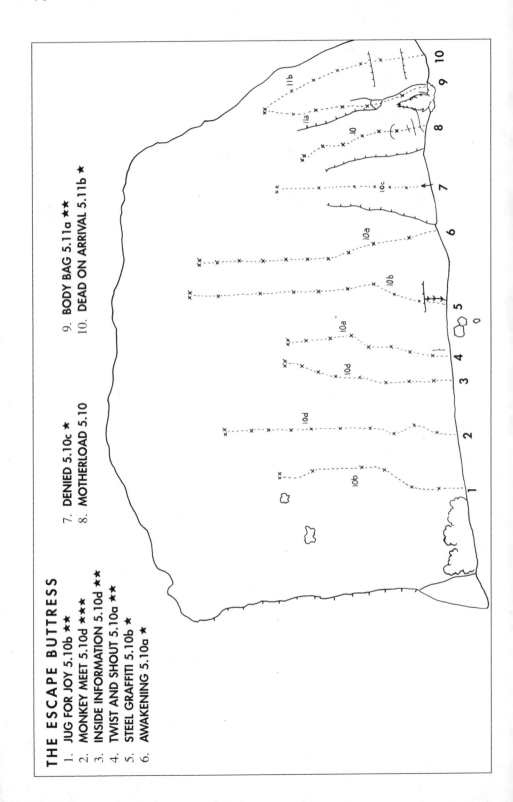

**THE ESCAPE BUTTRESS**
1. JUG FOR JOY 5.10b ★★
2. MONKEY MEET 5.10d ★★★
3. INSIDE INFORMATION 5.10d ★★
4. TWIST AND SHOUT 5.10a ★★
5. STEEL GRAFFITI 5.10b ★
6. AWAKENING 5.10a ★

7. DENIED 5.10c ★
8. MOTHERLOAD 5.10

9. BODY BAG 5.11a ★★
10. DEAD ON ARRIVAL 5.11b ★

## THE ESCAPE BUTTRESS

A high quality area. Pockets are plentiful, the routes rest at a good, steep angle, and the climbing is enjoyable. All this, plus a southern exposure combine to make this wall, one of the canyon's newer additions, also one of the most popular.

APPROACH: See the approach information in **The Hard Rock** section. From **The Hard Rock** area, follow a trail right (east) along a bench for 400 feet, passing the **White Wave Wall** at the halfway point, to the base of **The Escape Buttress**. Be careful on this traverse- there are several points where a thoughtless footstep could spell disaster.

1. **JUG FOR JOY 5.10b** ★★ "All the animals except man know that the principal business of life is to enjoy it." -Samuel Butler. Clean, positive climbing on the left side of the wall.
   FA: Brian Smoot and Jonathon Smoot.

2. **MONKEY MEET 5.10d** ★★★ This climb has been described as a route fit to be on **The Billboard**. A straight, unbroken line of pockets.
   FA: Brian Smoot and Jonathon Smoot.

3. **INSIDE INFORMATION 5.10d** ★★ Our insider's tip: invest in this route. Another classic pocket climb.
   FA: Brian Smoot.

4. **TWIST AND SHOUT 5.10a** ★★ "It's deja vu all over again." -Yogi Berra. More of the same good thing.
   FA: Brian Smoot and Vickie Smoot.

5. **STEEL GRAFFITI 5.10b** ★ This is the longest route on the wall. Once past the third bolt, the climbing is wonderfully moderate.
   FA: Brian Smoot.

6. **AWAKENING 5.10a** ★ An eye opener on the upper face.
   FA: Brian Smoot.

7. **DENIED 5.10c** ★ Starts with a bouldery crux and finishes with long runouts on easy ground.
   FA: Brain Smoot.

8. **MOTHERLOAD 5.10** Not in the same league as the other routes on this wall. Pockets that should clean up.
   FA: Brian Smoot.

9. **BODY BAG 5.11a** ★★ Offers unique and interesting climbing with no rests.
   FA: Brian Smoot and Kim Miller.

10. **DEAD ON ARRIVAL 5.11b** ★ Powerful, reachy and continuous.
    FA: guess who?

# NECROMANCER AND NARCOLEPSY

1. HARDER-FASTER 5.10b
2. NECROMANCER 5.10a ★
3. RETURN OF THE PRINCE 5.10
4. NARCOLEPSY 5.11b ★

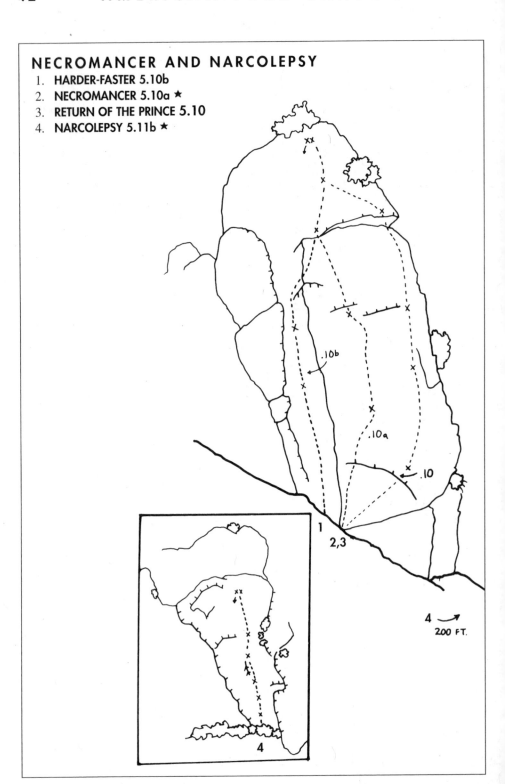

## NECROMANCER AND NARCOLEPSY

Actually two separate walls, but the parking is the same for both. The **Necromancer** area is a small formation hidden by trees. The **Narcolepsy** area is a south facing wall at the top of a talus slope.

APPROACH: Park 1.8 miles up canyon from the TCNM flagpole at a small pullout on the right (south) side of the road. This is the second pullout on the right .1 mile up canyon from **The Grey Cliffs** picnic area. To reach the **Necromancer** area, walk up canyon from the pullout and walk north into the trees on a trail that starts by a boulder. At the edge of a talus slope sits the **Necromancer** which can't be seen from the road although it is only 75 feet through the trees. See Aerial View page 69.

1. **HARDER-FASTER 5.10b** Join **Necromancer** after climbing past two bolts in a dihedral to the left. The rating reflects the climbing if the corner is avoided. However, if the corner is used, it is closer to 5.8.
   FA: Scott Unice and Tim Egbert.

2. **NECROMANCER 5.10a** ★ Four bolts of OK climbing.
   FA: Scott Unice and Bill Boyle.

3. **RETURN OF THE PRINCE 5.10** A boulder problem over the roof marks the start. Easier climbing above.

**Narcolepsy** is located 150-200 feet up the road from the **Necromancer** parking pullout. Scramble up loose dirt and scree for 150 feet to the base.

4. **NARCOLEPSY 5.11b** ★ Follow the steepest section of rock until near the top, then dodge right onto easier terrain.

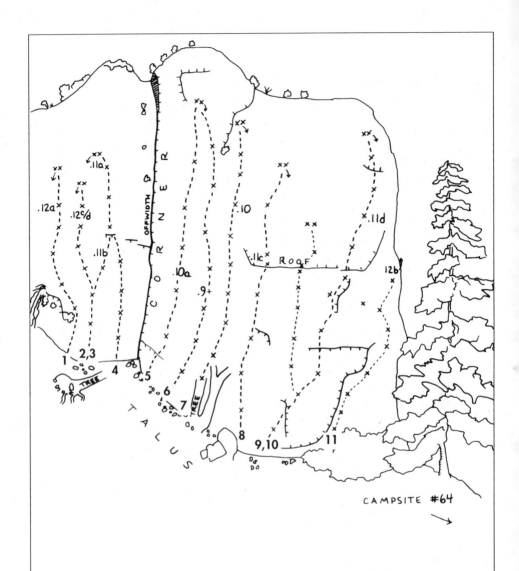

## DIVISION WALL - NORTH FACE

1. **LIQUID OXYGEN 5.12a ★★★**
2. **THE ABYSS 5.12c/d ★★**
3. **SHALLOW BEGINNING 5.11b ★★**
4. **DEEP END 5.11a ★★**
5. **BLACK HOLE 5.10a ★**
6. **PHYSICAL THERAPY 5.9+ ★★**
7. **TEENAGERS IN HEAT 5.10 ★**
8. **LITMUS TEST 5.11c ★★**
9. **PROJECT**
10. **SHARK CLUB 5.11d ★**
11. **SECRET WEAPON 5.12b ★**

## LITTLE MILL CAMPGROUND

The large campground 1.3 miles up from the Timpanogos Cave National Monument flagpole, has bundles of fine routes on some choice rock. The **Division Wall** is the single most popular crag in American Fork Canyon with a walloping 25 routes that climb through overhanging terrain on pockets and big edges. Quiet during the week, this campground transforms into a bustling hub of activity on holiday weekends. Wood smoke and the smell of frying bacon fill the air, and children run everywhere, wildly.

APPROACH: Park 2.3 miles up canyon from the TCNM flagpole at several small pullouts on the right (south) side of the road. This is the EXIT to the Little Mill Campground, and a tire shredder prevents motorized entry from this direction. Simply walk back through the campground until the desired campsite is reached. The order listed below flows from east to west; the first cliff you'll see as you walk down the Little Mill Campground road is the Division Wall. Car-to-climb time: five to ten minutes.

## DIVISION WALL

This wall is located just behind campsite 64. Pocketed and steep, it is hard to go wrong with any of the climbs here. It can become crowded on summer weekends, however.

APPROACH: See the approach information at the beginning of the Little Mill Campground section. Approach the **Division Wall** on the trail by the outhouse—don't cross through Campsite 64!

1. **LIQUID OXYGEN 5.12a** ★★★ Smoot's *piece de resistance* offering hard climbing between excellent pockets. A pumper finish leaves most climbers breathless. Popular.
   FA: Brian Smoot.

2. **THE ABYSS 5.12c/d** ★★ One of the most attempted hard routes in the canyon. Well protected climbing on small edges and pockets.
   FA: Merrill Bitter.

3. **SHALLOW BEGINNING 5.11b** ★★ Start on **The Abyss**, move up and right after two bolts and finish on **Deep End.** A good combo of strenuous and technical.
   FA: Merrill Bitter and Jeff Baldwin.

4. **DEEP END 5.11a** ★★ Climb the arête 8 feet left of the dihedral. The angle is deceptive—this is a pumper climb.
   FA: Bill Boyle.

5. **BLACK HOLE 5.10a** ★ Reachy and fashionably technical.
   FA: Brian Smoot.

6. **PHYSICAL THERAPY 5.9+** ★★ A fingery route with an exciting arête and interesting pockets that draw the crowds.
   FA: Brian and Jonathan Smoot.

7. **TEENAGERS IN HEAT 5.10** ★ "The suburbs have no charms to soothe the restless dreams of youth." -Neil Peart. Mega pockets give way to edges and more problematic climbing.
   FA: Brian and Jonathan Smoot.

8. **LITMUS TEST 5.11c** ★★ You'll probably change color after pulling the troubling roof.
   FA: Bill Boyle.

9. **PROJECT** Turns the roof to the right of Litmus Test. Looks good.

10. **SHARK CLUB 5.11d** ★ Membership has its dues. It has "recreational" climbing to a distinct crux. Nine bolts.
    FA: Conrad Anker and Doug Heinrich.

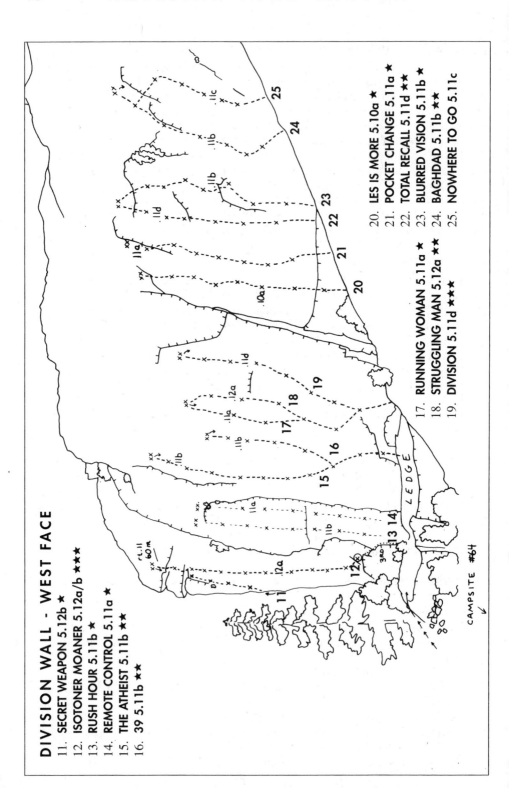

DIVISION WALL - WEST FACE
11. SECRET WEAPON 5.12b ★
12. ISOTONER MOANER 5.12a/b ★★★
13. RUSH HOUR 5.11b ★
14. REMOTE CONTROL 5.11a ★
15. THE ATHEIST 5.11b ★★
16. 39 5.11b ★★
17. RUNNING WOMAN 5.11a ★
18. STRUGGLING MAN 5.12a ★★
19. DIVISION 5.11d ★★★
20. LES IS MORE 5.10a ★
21. POCKET CHANGE 5.11a ★
22. TOTAL RECALL 5.11d ★★
23. BLURRED VISION 5.11b ★
24. BAGHDAD 5.11b ★★
25. NOWHERE TO GO 5.11c

CAMPSITE #64

11. **SECRET WEAPON 5.12b** ★ A lengthy tour of the **Division Wall.** A hard sloper move is the crux, followed by single handed pulls. The upper face is great. This climb may have as many as 17 bolts. Bring two ropes or a 60 meter to get off.
FA: Doug Heinrich and Bill Boyle.

12. **ISOTONER MOANER 5.12a/b** ★★★ Belay 15 feet up on a ledge (optional). Long, with several distinct and varied sections.
FA: Bill Boyle.

13. **RUSH HOUR 5.11b** ★ Climbs smooth bullet-proof rock 20 feet right of **Isotoner Moaner.** Neat moves and a reachy crux lead to evenly spaced pocket pulling. Will get better with time as the holds clean up.
FA: Brian Smoot.

14. **REMOTE CONTROL 5.11a** ★ Clamber up the thin flake on great rock to the steep pocketed wall above. Slight runout to chains.
FA: Brian Smoot.

15. **THE ATHEIST 5.11b** ★★ Thin holds at the top. You've got to believe if you're going to achieve.
FA: Bill Boyle.

16. **39 5.11b** ★★ "It was the best of times, it was the worst of times." Charles Dickens. Thirty-ninth was a birthday to remember. Continuously fun climbing. Clipping into the chains is an eye opener.
FA: Bill Boyle.

17. **RUNNING WOMAN 5.11a** ★ A sprint to the chains that seems a bit squeezed. Blowing the third clip would be really bad.
FA: Conrad Anker.

18. **STRUGGLING MAN 5.12a** ★★ Most feel destitute of finger strength near the top. A hard clip off the big sloping pocket up high is a gas.
FA: Boone Speed and Bill Boyle.

19. **DIVISION 5.11d** ★★★ "If you come to a fork in the road, take it." -Yogi Berra. An archetypal American Fork route. Quality.
FA: Boone Speed and Bill Boyle.

20. **LES IS MORE 5.10a** ★ Climb the face just right of the big crack on the **Division Wall**. Pockets give way to stems at the top of the route.
FA: Les Ellison and Brian Smoot.

21. **POCKET CHANGE 5.11a** ★ Our two cents worth: the crux is the very last move, or two.
FA: Brian Smoot and Les Ellison.

22. **TOTAL RECALL 5.11d** ★★ An action packed adventure. Tricky sidepulls are the norm on this Schwarzenegger-type route.
FA: Gordon Douglass and Eric Stroud.

23. **BLURRED VISION 5.11b** ★ Some unique "handlebar holds," and hidden pockets that require a sharp eye.
FA: Brian Smoot and Les Ellison.

24. **BAGHDAD 5.11b** ★★ Enter Operation Desert Storm. Evenly spaced pockets, continuous climbing and long reaches are the attributes of this route.
FA: Brian Smoot.

25. **NOWHERE TO GO 5.11c** A bouldery crux out some very steep terrain.
FA: Brian Smoot.

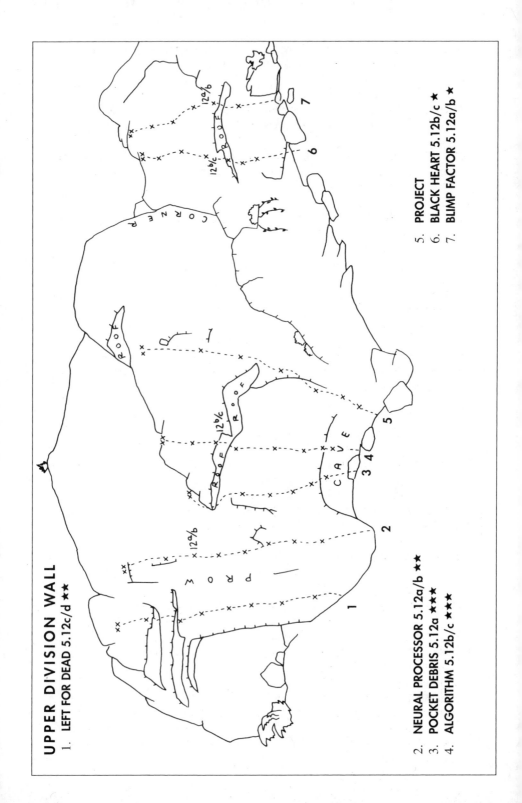

UPPER DIVISION WALL
1. LEFT FOR DEAD 5.12c/d ★★

2. NEURAL PROCESSOR 5.12a/b ★★
3. POCKET DEBRIS 5.12a ★★★
4. ALGORITHM 5.12b/c ★★★

5. PROJECT
6. BLACK HEART 5.12b/c ★
7. BLIMP FACTOR 5.12a/b ★

## UPPER DIVISION WALL

Pockets, pockets, pockets. This wall is steep, pumpy, and riddled with holes. Although west facing, shade prevails here most of the day. Climbing at the **Upper Division Wall** requires responsibility and maturity. Any rock, no matter how small, that rolls down from this cliff, could injure or kill someone climbing directly below on the **Division Wall**. Great care must be taken, dogs should be left behind, and climbers should stay away from the edge. If you are not capable of controlling yourself or your partners, don't visit this wall!

APPROACH: See the approach information at the beginning of the Little Mill Campground section. From campsite 64, walk around to the left of the **Division Wall**, past **Liquid Oxygen**, and continue up the talus on the remnants of a switchbacking trail. The trail cuts steeply to the right as soon as it is possible to get on top of the wall that has formed the right margin of the talus. Follow this trail to the base of the wall. PLEASE BE EXTREMELY CAREFUL WITH ROCK FALL.

1. **LEFT FOR DEAD 5.12c/d ★★** The crux is bouldery and the roofs are cool. Expect to be perplexed.
   FA: Bill Blosser, Craig Canezel and Mark Liebman.

2. **NEURAL PROCESSOR 5.12a/b ★★** The loose-looking block above the third bolt is a heart stopper, but the pockets make up for it. Strenuous and desperate to the end, this route is not a giveaway.
   FA: Bill Boyle.

3. **POCKET DEBRIS 5.12a ★★★** Plentiful pockets that require powerful pulling.
   FA: Craig Canezel.

4. **ALGORITHM 5.12b/c ★★★** Sublime.
   FA: Bill Boyle.

5. **PROJECT** The first two bolts are in bad rock.

6. **BLACK HEART 5.12b/c ★** Pulling the roof gets right to the heart of the matter. The left line up the steep wall.
   FA: Bill Boyle.

7. **BLIMP FACTOR 5.12a/b ★** "He must have had a magnificent build before his stomach went in for a career of its own." -Margaret Halsey. An easier line over the roof for the "gravity impaired."
   FA: Bill Boyle.

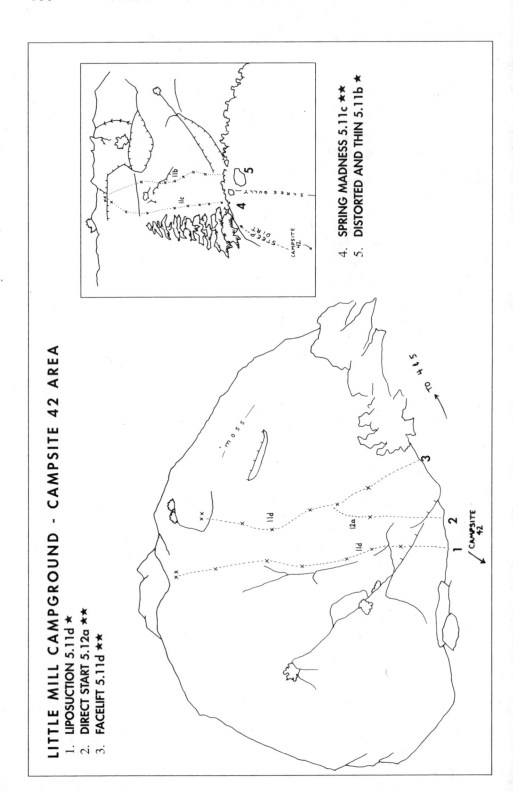

LITTLE MILL CAMPGROUND - CAMPSITE 42 AREA
1. LIPOSUCTION 5.11d ★
2. DIRECT START 5.12a ★★
3. FACELIFT 5.11d ★★
4. SPRING MADNESS 5.11c ★★
5. DISTORTED AND THIN 5.11b ★

## CAMPSITE 42

There are two separate walls behind campsite 42. The lower wall is the **Facelift** area, where several well-liked routes climb good rock on edges and flakes. The upper wall sees less traffic, although the route quality remains consistent.

APPROACH: See the approach information at the beginning of the Little Mill Campground section.

There are several good boulder problems located on the large pocketed boulder between campsite 42 and the **Facelift** wall. The difficulties range from warmups to a V7 traverse.

1. **LIPOSUCTION 5.11d** ★ Climbing near the seam with a low, bouldery crux. A long reach at the second bolt is made easier by a stem to the left. This was one of the first top ropes in the canyon.

2. **DIRECT START 5.12a** ★★ Straightens out the start of **Facelift**, joining at the second bolt. Beware the first jug, it is loose.

3. **FACELIFT 5.11d** ★★ "God hath given you one face, and you make yourself another." -William Shakespeare. The climber is faced with a conundrum just past the 4th bolt. FA: Bart Dahneke.

The following routes are up and right 200 feet from **Facelift**.

4. **SPRING MADNESS 5.11c** ★★ Excellent climbing with one big runout. FA: Bill Boyle and Boone Speed.

5. **DISTORTED AND THIN 5.11b** ★ Good climbing on the line of bolts to the right. FA: Bill Boyle and Boone Speed.

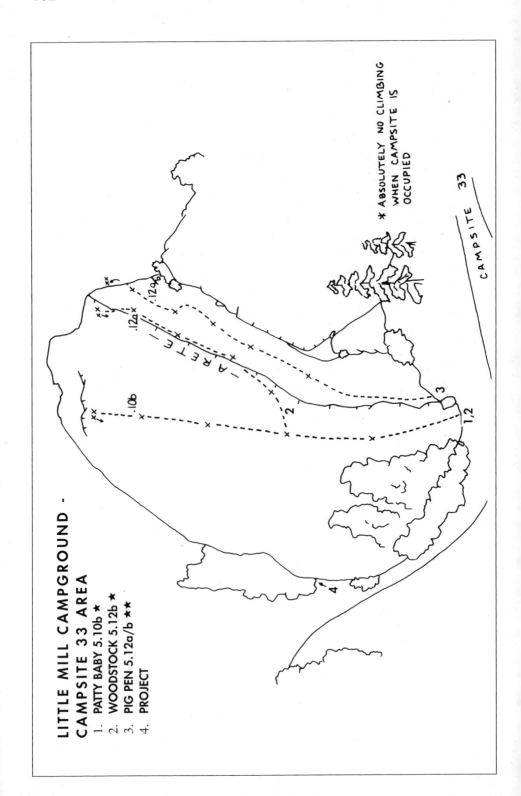

LITTLE MILL CAMPGROUND -
CAMPSITE 33 AREA
1. PATTY BABY 5.10b ★
2. WOODSTOCK 5.12b ★
3. PIG PEN 5.12a/b ★★
4. PROJECT

★ ABSOLUTELY NO CLIMBING
WHEN CAMPSITE IS
OCCUPIED

CAMPSITE 33

## CAMPSITE 33

The following routes are located at campsite 33 and offer great pocket climbing. An agreement between climbers and the forest service has allowed climbing to continue at this site for now, so please respect the efforts made by all persons involved. POSITIVELY NO CLIMBING WHEN CAMPSITE 33 IS OCCUPIED.

APPROACH: See the approach information at the beginning of the Little Mill Campground Section.

1. **PATTY BABY 5.10b** ★ Good climbing on shallow pockets with a courageous second clip. Unfortunately, the scene of several accidents.
   FA: Bill Boyle.

2. **WOODSTOCK 5.12b** ★ The crux involves a full body throw.
   FA: Kelly Oldroid

3. **PIG PEN 5.12a/b** ★★ A burly move concludes this popular route.
   FA: Boone Speed.

4. **PROJECT** A four bolt line up the blank east face.

## NORTH FORK CRAG

So far only one route is located here. North facing, this wall is nice on hot summer days.

APPROACH: 2.5 miles up canyon from the TCNM flagpole, the road forks. Take the left fork and park at the first pullout on the left (west) side of the road. Make the killer 50 foot hike to reach the wall. See Aerial View page 14.

1. **BAD DREAMS 5.12** Follow six bolts to chain anchors. This route seems to see little action. No topo.

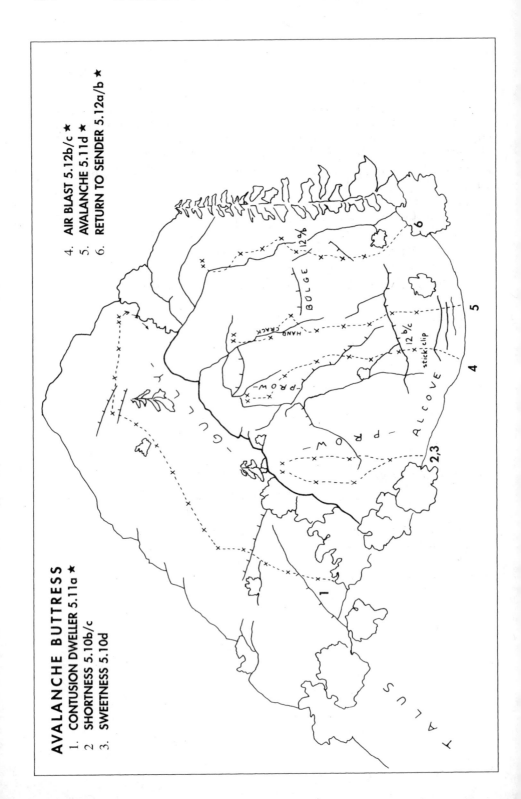

AVALANCHE BUTTRESS
1. CONTUSION DWELLER 5.11a ★
2. SHORTNESS 5.10b/c
3. SWEETNESS 5.10d
4. AIR BLAST 5.12b/c ★
5. AVALANCHE 5.11d ★
6. RETURN TO SENDER 5.12a/b ★

## AVALANCHE BUTTRESS

The **Avalanche Buttress** is a collection of six routes of varying difficulty. Although the approach is not long, a remote atmosphere pervades these walls, and it is rare to see another climbing party here. The main wall is steep with bulges, and two prominent crack lines split the face. The rock quality varies, and pockets are the exception. Layaways, sidepulls and edges provide most of the upward movement. The wall faces south and a bit east, so it catches sun until late afternoon. See Aerial View page 14.

APPROACH: 2.5 miles up canyon from the TCNM flagpole, the road forks. Take the left fork (North Fork) and park after 1.1 miles at a small pullout on the right (east) side of the road. This is just past the entrance to Martin Campground, and is actually the parking for site number five. If there is someone camped here, continue up the road to the next pullout. You will notice a huge avalanche gully coming into the road from the left (west). Walk up this gully, over a mass of downed trees and dead wood from an avalanche in the spring of 1993. As of this writing, all approach possibilities seem about the same—just try and find the path of least resistance through the avalanche debris. As the brush grows back, one path should become evident. The approach takes 20 to 25 minutes, and the wall is the first rock encountered on the right (north).

1. **CONTUSION DWELLER 5.11a** ★ The strangest line in American Fork Canyon. Climb up and right on a grand tour of roofs, slabs, and ledge systems. Bring several long runners for the fifth and sixth bolts.
   FA: Tim Roberts.

2. **SHORTNESS 5.10b/c** A shorty indeed. Shares the first bolt with sweetness and sports a scary second clip.
   FA: Tim Roberts.

3. **SWEETNESS 5.10d** Inobvious climbing with a dangerous second clip.
   FA: Tim Roberts.

4. **AIR BLAST 5.12b/c** ★ Your arms are what will feel blasted. Stick clip the first bolt and boulder to the second. The upper section is steep and exciting.
   FA: Tim Roberts.

5. **AVALANCHE 5.11d** ★ The left crack. Good holds lead to handjams. Taping up is recommended.
   FA: Tim Roberts.

6. **RETURN TO SENDER 5.12a/b** ★ Several burly moves are followed by a wild series of rounded layaways. The final sprint to the anchors is not for the meek—it is very sporty.
   FA: Tim Roberts.

**Atrocious [5.11c]**, Rock Canyon

# ROCK CANYON

Located east of the city of Provo is an impressive canyon full of huge rock walls. Rock Canyon is a haven for the explorer, rock hound and climber. The climbing is centered in two separate areas of the canyon where the rock types are vastly different: technical quartzite at the mouth of the canyon, and steep limestone sport climbing near the canyon's midsection.

Although small in stature, the quality of the quartzite is great and the routes are big fun to climb. The rock tends to be slick (even for quartzite) and is fractured into beautiful cracks and joints. The best quality rock is on the **Green Monster Slab**, **Bolt Slab**, **Red Slab** and **The Kitchen**. Route lengths vary from short problems in **The Kitchen**, to 130 feet on the **Green Monster** and **Ed and Terry Walls**. There are even three pitch routes on the **Bad Bananas Wall**. The lower canyon's unique echo propensities amplify every noise. And weekends can sound as if there were a concert happening nearby. Unfortunately, this area is also a hangout for "headbangers" and partiers. Graffiti, broken glass and beer cans litter the parking lots and lower cliffs.

The limestone further up the canyon is a different experience. Many hours of climbing can be enjoyed without seeing another person. The canyon bottom is lush with trees and foliage, and the stream flows about half the year. The climbing is generally on vertical to slightly overhanging fins of rock, requiring more technique than brawn. **The Projects** and **The Threshold**, however, are mostly overhanging and power oriented. With the exception of **The Cemetery** and the **Mass Murder Wall**, the rock quality of the limestone here is excellent.

The geology of this canyon is fascinating. The rocks have been subjected to big-time stress and strain, creating steeply dipping beds, folds and faults. The quartzite at the mouth is Cambrian, about 590 million years in age. As you walk up the canyon into younger rocks, twisting beds of Mississippian dolomite and limestone (about 370 million years old) plunge toward the stream from high on the canyon walls. To geologists this is an overturned anticline. To hikers and climbers it seems a maze which craves exploring.

## HOW TO GET THERE

From the north, drive along I-15 to exit 272, 12th So. State in Orem. Drive east on this road as it eventually turns into University Parkway. Turn L on 550 W (also 2230 N) in Provo. Continue on 2230 N, then turn L on North Temple Drive. Drive toward the canyon on this road, taking a L at 2300 N and then a R at a Y intersection. Drive up and park where the pavement ends. The Turnaround parking area is the first parking, with a boulder in the middle. The Waterhouse parking is near the end of the road, across from a small building.

From the south, exit off I-15 at exit 266. This is the exit for University Avenue and Utah Highway 189 north. Drive north on University Avenue and turn right on 2230 N. Follow this to the Provo Temple and turn left on North Temple Drive. Drive towards the canyon on this road, taking a L at 2300 N, and then a R a the Y intersection. Drive up and park where the pavement ends. The Turnaround parking area is the first parking, with a boulder in the middle. The Waterhouse parking is near the end of the road, across from a small building.

It is possible to drive directly from Rock Canyon to American Fork Canyon without a lengthy side trip to the Interstate. Simply backtrack the northern approach described on page 107 to the corner of University Parkway and State Street. (This is the corner of 1300 South and Highway 89). Turn right (north) and follow State Street to the town of Pleasant Grove. North of Pleasant Grove is an easy to miss intersection with Highway 146. Turn right on 146 and follow it to the mouth of American Fork Canyon.

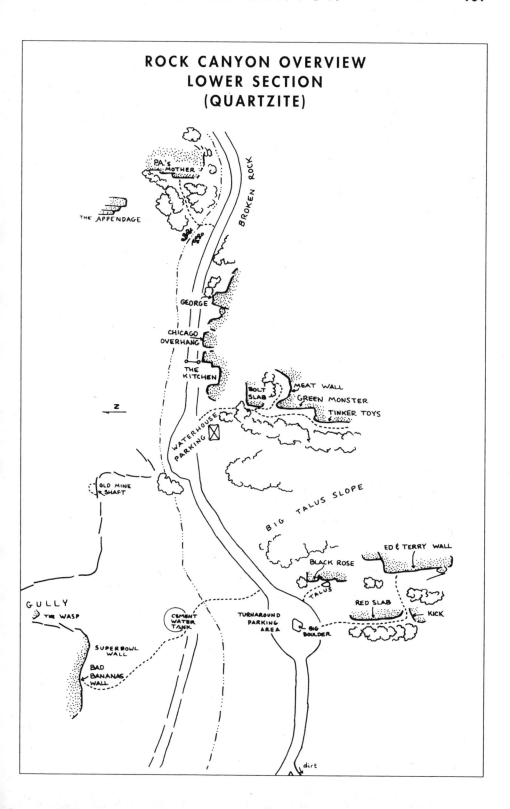

ROCK CANYON OVERVIEW
LOWER SECTION
(QUARTZITE)

PA's MOTHER

THE APPENDAGE

BROKEN ROCK

GEORGE

CHICAGO OVERHANG

THE KITCHEN

BOLT SLAB

MEAT WALL

GREEN MONSTER

TINKER TOYS

WATERHOUSE PARKING

N

OLD MINE SHAFT

BIG TALUS SLOPE

ED & TERRY WALL

BLACK ROSE

TALUS

RED SLAB

KICK

GULLY

THE WASP

CEMENT WATER TANK

TURNAROUND PARKING AREA

BIG BOULDER

SUPERBOWL WALL

BAD BANANAS WALL

dirt

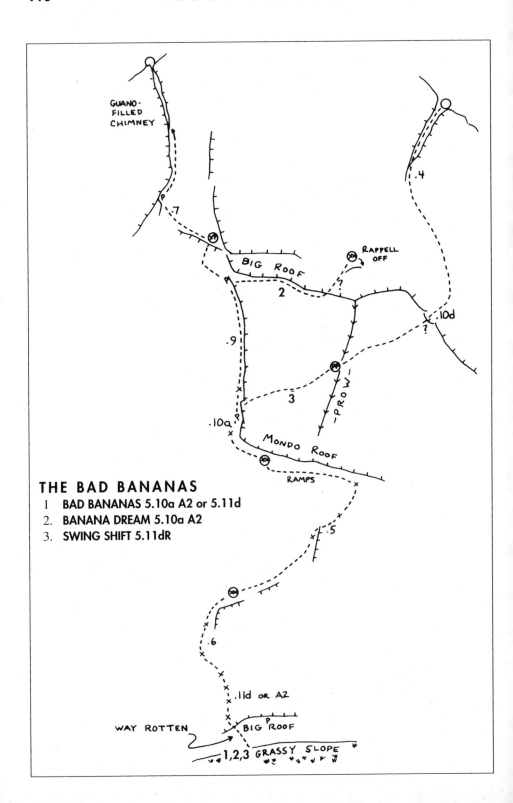

GUANO-
FILLED
CHIMNEY

.4

.7

BIG ROOF

RAPPELL
OFF

2

10d
?

.9

PROW

3

.10a

MONDO ROOF

RAMPS

**THE BAD BANANAS**
1. BAD BANANAS 5.10a A2 or 5.11d
2. BANANA DREAM 5.10a A2
3. SWING SHIFT 5.11dR

.5

.6

.11d or A2

WAY ROTTEN

BIG ROOF

1,2,3 GRASSY SLOPE

## ROCK CANYON QUARTZITE

## THE BAD BANANAS

**The Bad Bananas** wall is the largest quartzite wall in Rock Canyon. The three routes that grace its flanks are exposed, strenuous, and spectacular. Unfortunately, the rock is rotten, the gear is dubious, and the lines are hard to discern. Climbers should only attempt a route on this wall if it is well within their ability, and if they have considerable experience with loose, rotten rock. Great care must also be taken to protect the rope from sharp edges, which seem to be everywhere. Needless to say, **The Bad Bananas** wall does not attract much attention. However, if a climbing party is well prepared, fully competent, and extremely careful, a successful ascent can be a rewarding experience.

APPROACH: From the Turnaround parking area, a quick hop across the stream reaches a road and a huge fenced-in cement water tank. If the stream is too high, simply drive to the water tank via the left fork of the road, several hundred feet down canyon. Walk up a steep road to the right (east) of the water tower for 100 feet, traverse left (west) on a trail which diagonals up and left (west) for 300 feet. This deposits you near the base of the **Superbowl Wall.** Traverse 100 feet left (west) along the base of the wall to reach the start of the routes. The wall is characterized by several large roofs, including one down near the base of the wall. See Aerial View page 109.

1  **BAD BANANAS 5.10a A2 or 5.11d** Locate the bolt ladder to the left of the large roof near the base of the wall. This marks the start for all three routes. **Bad Bananas** is the "easiest" route to reach the top of the wall. Beware of rope drag on the second pitch, and as always, be suspect of all rock.

2. **BANANA DREAM 5.10a A2** This is actually a variation off **Bad Bananas** that goes nowhere, but has lots of exposure. The exact location of the belay/rappel at the top of pitch three is not known, but it is there. Be warned that to venture any higher than this rappel station could be fatal.

3. **SWING SHIFT 5.11dR** This is the free line up the wall. Free climb the initial bolt ladder, and continue up **Bad Bananas.** After rounding the corner on the third pitch of **Bad Bananas**, traverse right to an exposed belay. The fourth pitch continues the rightward traverse, turns the roof and eventually gains a chimney and the summit. Whew!
FA: Mark Ward and Kim Miller, 197?

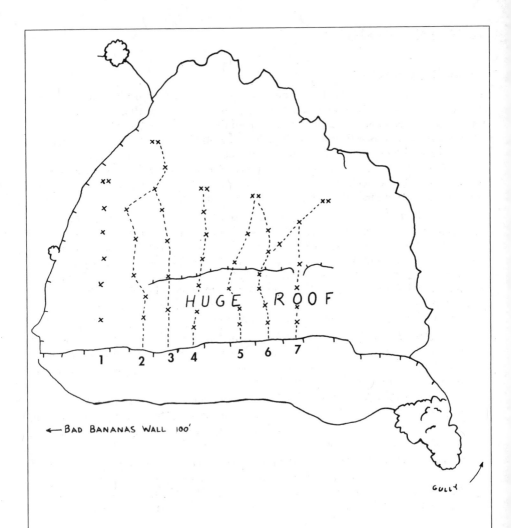

← Bad Bananas Wall 100'

GULLY

## SUPERBOWL WALL
1. PROJECT
2. OBSESSIVE TENDENCIES 5.11a
3. EVEREST 101 5.11a/b ★
4. THE HIGH, HARD ONE 5.11b/c ★
5. SIMPLE SIMON 5.11b ★★
6. SMASH THE POSER 5.12a ★
7. PROJECT

## SUPERBOWL WALL

Steep and juggy are the words for this wall. Big roofs, big holds and big reaches equal big fun. Expect some dirty holds as these routes are still new. They should improve with more traffic. Facing due south, this wall is an oven on sunny winter days.

APPROACH: From the Turnaround parking area, a quick hop across the stream reaches a road and a huge fenced-in cement water tank. If the stream is too high, simply drive to the water tank via the left fork of the road several hundred feet down canyon. Walk up the steep dirt road right (east) of the water tank for 100 feet, traverse left (west) on a steep trail that diagonals up and left (west) for another 300 feet to these very overhung routes. See Aerial View page 109.

1. **PROJECT** Climb the wall to the left of the roofs.

2. **OBSESSIVE TENDENCIES 5.11a** Smaller, weird edges and a tricky traverse.
   FA: Brian Team.

3. **EVEREST 101 5.11a/b** ★ Because it's there. A boulder problem start gives way to better holds, followed by some slopers at the top.
   FA: Darren Knezek.

4. **THE HIGH, HARD ONE 5.11b/c** ★ Reach high. Pull hard. Devious moves, a hard-to-see pocket, and all while the clock is ticking.
   FA: Darren Knezek.

5. **SIMPLE SIMON 5.11b** ★★ The only simple thing about this roof is missing the key hidden hold. Mostly good jugs.
   FA: Jeff Pedersen.

6. **SMASH THE POSER 5.12a** ★ "A photograph is a secret about a secret. The more it tells you the less you know." -Diane Arbus. A hard boulder problem which requires serious arm power.
   FA: Jeff Pedersen.

7. **PROJECT** Climbs out the right side of the roof.

Climbing at the **Superbowl Wall. Simple Simon** [5.11b]

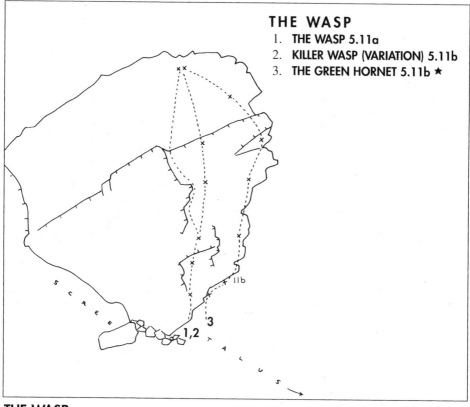

**THE WASP**
1. THE WASP 5.11a
2. KILLER WASP (VARIATION) 5.11b
3. THE GREEN HORNET 5.11b ★

## THE WASP

Two routes and a variation reside on this west facing chunk of quartzite. The routes are steep and pumpy. The rock is shattered, sharp, and a bit loose.

APPROACH: From the Turnaround parking area, a quick hop across the stream reaches a road and a huge fenced-in cement water tank. If the stream is too high, simply drive to the water tank via the left fork of the road, several hundred feet down canyon. To the right (east) of the water tank and up high is a gully. Several trails leave from the vicinity of the water tank and head toward the gully. Walk up the gully and turn left (west) at the first dark quartzite wall on the left (west). Walk west on the ledge system 100 feet and round the corner to find these routes. See Aerial View page 109.

1. **THE WASP 5.11a** Clip the first bolt off the big talus blocks. Step down and right of the bolt to start climbing. Once past the second bolt, its a buzz to the top.
   FA: Tim Hannig and Darren Knezek.

2. **KILLER WASP (VARIATION) 5.11b** A contrived variation. Climb **The Wasp**, but don't use the small corner to the left.
   FA: Tim Hannig and Darren Knezek.

3. **THE GREEN HORNET 5.11b ★** Climb the right arête over several visor-like roofs. The rock is somewhat shattered.
   FA: Tim Hannig and Darren Knezek

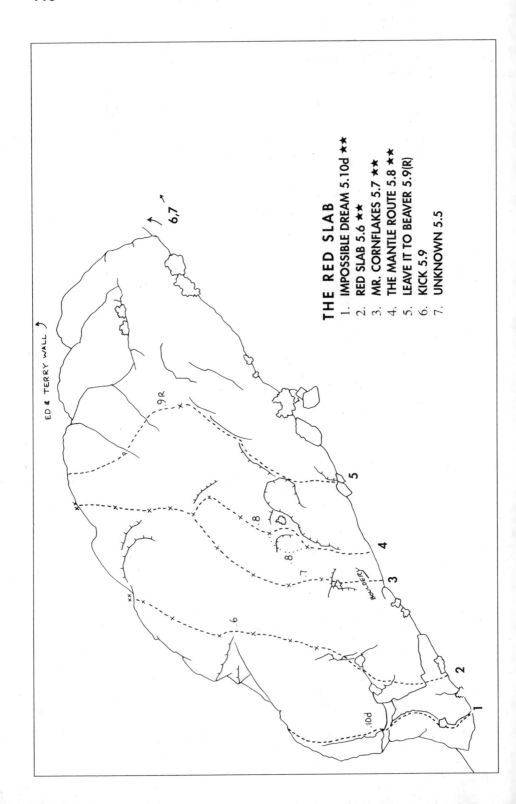

THE RED SLAB
1. IMPOSSIBLE DREAM 5.10d ★★
2. RED SLAB 5.6 ★★
3. MR. CORNFLAKES 5.7 ★★
4. THE MANTLE ROUTE 5.8 ★★
5. LEAVE IT TO BEAVER 5.9(R)
6. KICK 5.9
7. UNKNOWN 5.5

## THE RED SLAB

**The Red Slab** rests at an angle that is perfect for beginning leaders. Most routes are bolt protected and the rock quality is excellent. With an easy approach and varied moves, **The Red Slab is** home to considerable traffic. Although bolted, several routes require gear other than quickdraws, so the rack should not be left behind.

APPROACH: From the Turnaround parking area, walk south up a steep trail to reach the base of the wall. See Aerial View page 109.

1. **IMPOSSIBLE DREAM 5.10d ★★** Climb the short thin crack at the lowest point of the wall. Turning the roof is a real challenge, but is made safer by packing along many small to medium nuts.

2. **RED SLAB 5.6 ★★** A long route with varied and interesting moves. Several nut placements protect the climbing up to the first bolt.

3. **MR. CORNFLAKES 5.7 ★★** Long and continuous, with a bouldery start that guards the first bolt.

4. **THE MANTLE ROUTE 5.8 ★★** The name is a clue. Fun moves and good rock. This route shares the finish with **Mr. Cornflakes.**

5. **LEAVE IT TO BEAVER 5.9(R)** Most people just leave it alone. Not a route for the faint of heart. Expect long runouts and shaky protection. A small tcu or tri-cam is helpful.

6. **KICK 5.9** At the upper end of the **Red Slab** is a north-facing alcove split by a wide left-leaning crack. Climb the crack, clipping a pin to the left. With a large friend in place at the lip, turn the roof and continue up the low angled, mossy corner above.

7. **UNKNOWN 5.5** From **Kick**, walk west 20 feet then uphill (south) 150 feet to the start of the route in a scooped out area on the west face of the wall. Five bolts lead to the anchors. Mossy.

## ED AND TERRY WALL

The **Ed and Terry Wall** is the second largest outcrop in Rock Canyon. The west face is comprised of good, clean rock, split by several cracks. Although the concentration of high quality routes is greater here than any other wall in the canyon, the **Ed and Terry** area is visited less frequently because of the longer approach (five minutes!) and the serious reputation of several routes. For those seeking the best climbs in the canyon, this is the place.

APPROACH: Approach as for the **Red Slab**. Continue walking to the uphill end (south end) of the **Red Slab** and scramble up a series of ledge systems and traverses to reach the base of the **Ed and Terry Wall**. It is also possible to scramble up ledges at the north end of the **Red Slab**. Care should be taken on either approach. See Aerial View page 109.

1. **I'M NOT LICHEN THIS 5.7 ★** There is some lichen, but the climbing is still good. Shudder past some devious moves to an exposed belay.

2. **NORTH CHIMNEY 5.7** Climb the chimney that is formed by the inside corner to the right of **I'm Not Lichen This**.

3. **NORTH CRACK 5.9 ★** The left-leaning finger crack between **North Chimney** and **Inner Limits** cuts a clean line through the steep face.

4. **INNER LIMITS 5.11 ★★** This heart-racer climbs the north arête, passing a pin and three bolts before escaping right to the lower angled west face. Begin by climbing up **North Crack** and traversing right to the arête. Expect a good pump and wild exposure.

5. **CAPTURED FOR RAPTURE 5.10d(R) ★★** A variation start to **Edge of Night,** this route pulls two roofs near the left hand edge of the west face. Luckily, the crux is well protected.

6. **EDGE OF KNIGHT 5.10(R) ★★★** This classic begins with unprotected 5.8 climbing. Airy moves on the upper face make a lasting impression.

7. **EDGE OF THE WORLD 5.8(R) ★★** The start is runout and the upper face can be a puzzler. After a successful climb, most leaders feel as though they are on top of the world.

8. **FLAKES 5.7 ★★** A fine route that tackles the flake system to the left of the **Main Crack.** Bring along extra wired nuts and an appetite for fun.

9. **MAIN CRACK 5.7 ★★** Another **Ed and Terry** classic that follows the most obvious line up the face. A good selection of two to three and a half inch protection is real handy, as is a solid crack climbing technique.

10. **ROACHES ON A FACE 5.10d ★★** A sporty undertaking that climbs small edges up a clean face and then turns a roof at mid-height. Several TCU's are good for reducing the runouts between bolts, and the staying power of a roach is also a coveted trait.

11. **NO WAY IN HELL 5.8 ★** The interesting slot half-way up the wall is awkward for some people, but the climbing is good fun.

12. **REAL McCOY 5.7 ★★** This is it...the real thing. A clean swath up the right side of the wall is the attraction. Four bolts and quality climbing wrap up another hyper-route.

The following two routes are located on the overhanging east face of the Ed and Terry Wall. Follow the regular approach to I'm Not Lichen This, then turn the corner on ledge systems and traverse south to reach the wall.

13. **CLOSE YOUR EYES AND FANTASIZE 5.12c/d** ★★ A Rock Canyon test piece. Most climbers have to fantasize holds on the face. For the full fantasy, zip up past the the bolts to the chain anchor.
FA: Boone Speed 1987

14. **NEOSYMIAN THUGS 5.11d T.R.** ★ Climb the arête to the right of **Close Your Eyes and Fantasize**.
FA: Jeff Pedersen 1987

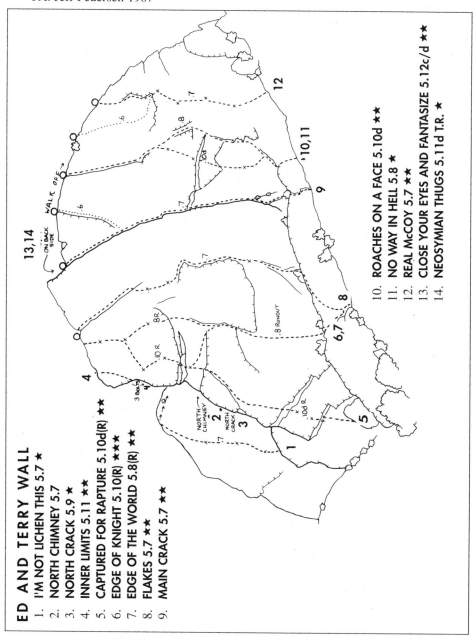

**ED AND TERRY WALL**
1. I'M NOT LICHEN THIS 5.7 ★
2. NORTH CHIMNEY 5.7
3. NORTH CRACK 5.9 ★
4. INNER LIMITS 5.11 ★★
5. CAPTURED FOR RAPTURE 5.10d(R) ★★
6. EDGE OF KNIGHT 5.10(R) ★★★
7. EDGE OF THE WORLD 5.8(R) ★★
8. FLAKES 5.7 ★★
9. MAIN CRACK 5.7 ★★
10. ROACHES ON A FACE 5.10d ★★
11. NO WAY IN HELL 5.8 ★
12. REAL McCOY 5.7 ★★
13. CLOSE YOUR EYES AND FANTASIZE 5.12c/d ★★
14. NEOSYMIAN THUGS 5.11d T.R. ★

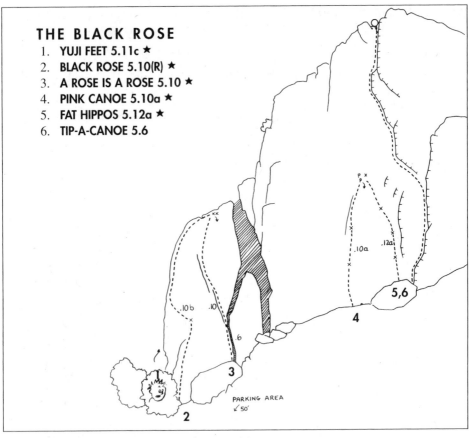

**THE BLACK ROSE**
1. YUJI FEET 5.11c ★
2. BLACK ROSE 5.10(R) ★
3. A ROSE IS A ROSE 5.10 ★
4. PINK CANOE 5.10a ★
5. FAT HIPPOS 5.12a ★
6. TIP-A-CANOE 5.6

## THE BLACK ROSE

Within fifty feet of the road and easily seen by spectators, **The Black Rose** Area sees constant action. The rock is smooth and the routes tend to be difficult, rounded outings that require thought and grace.

APPROACH: Are you serious? From the Turnaround parking area, walk fifty feet East up the talus slope to reach the wall. Flip-flops are fine for this approach. See Aerial View page 109.

1.  **YUJI FEET 5.11c ★** Try to stay on the left side of the arête for the most value. Even if you bail out and go onto the right side of the arête, the climbing is still fun.

2.  **BLACK ROSE 5.10(R) ★** A scary route with limited protection. Although the crux is protected by a bolt, the upper moves require steady nerves.

3.  **A ROSE IS A ROSE 5.10 ★** The devious crack line to the right of **Black Rose.**

4.  **PINK CANOE 5.10a ★** A slippery route that requires thin liebacks up an offset seam. Short.

5.  **FAT HIPPOS 5.12a ★** A definite weight watchers route. Thin moves and anorexic holds spit out the steak and eggs crowd.

6.  **TIP-A-CANOE 5.6** The long, somewhat broken (and loose) corner that stretches to the top of the wall.

Kim Miller leading **Erase Your Face [5.10d] Green Monter Slab**

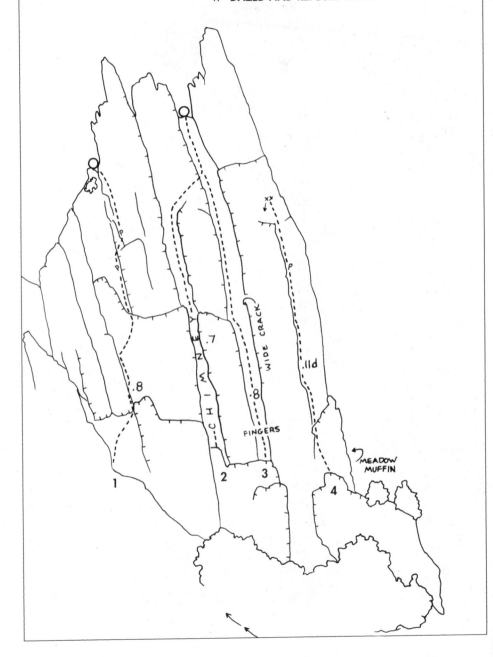

BOLT SLAB NORTH FACE
1   DANCE OF THE PREGNANT WILDEBEAST 5.8 ★
2.  CHIMNEY ROUTE 5.7 ★
3.  DOUBLE JAM 5.8 ★★
4.  DAZED AND REFUSED 5.11d ★

## THE GREEN MONSTER SLAB AREA

This is the best section of cliff in the canyon and has numerous high quality routes. It comprises **Bolt Slab North Face**, **Bolt Slab West Face**, **Meat Wall**, **Green Monster Slab** and **Tinker Toys Slab.**

APPROACH: Park at the Waterhouse parking area. Just past the waterhouse, and before reaching the **Kitchen**, a trail cuts off of the road to the south. This trail climbs a short scree slope and then traverses the bases of **Bolt Slab**, **Green Monster Slab** and **Tinker Toys** at the uphill end. The total approach is a whopping thirty seconds to a minute ordeal. See Aerial View page 109.

## THE NORTH FACES

## BOLT SLAB NORTH FACE

The following four routes are located on the steep north face of the **Bolt Slab**. These cracks face the road and remain in the shade even in the hottest weather.

APPROACH: See the approach information for **Green Monster Slab** Area.

1   **DANCE OF THE PREGNANT WILDEBEAST 5.8** ★ A steep route that links together the weaknesses on the left side of the face. The rock at the bottom is rotten, but it improves higher up on the climb. The hand crack after the roof is an awkward size for those climbers with normal to large hands.

2.  **CHIMNEY ROUTE 5.7** ★ The chimney line up the center of the face is best saved for those days when one is feeling thin.

3.  **DOUBLE JAM 5.8** ★★ Strenuous finger cracks at the bottom relent to easier climbing above. The protection is good.

4.  **DAZED AND REFUSED 5.11d** ★ A powerful route up the tips crack near the arête. A test piece that denies most climbers on their first attempt. Small to medium nuts and tcu's are all that is needed.

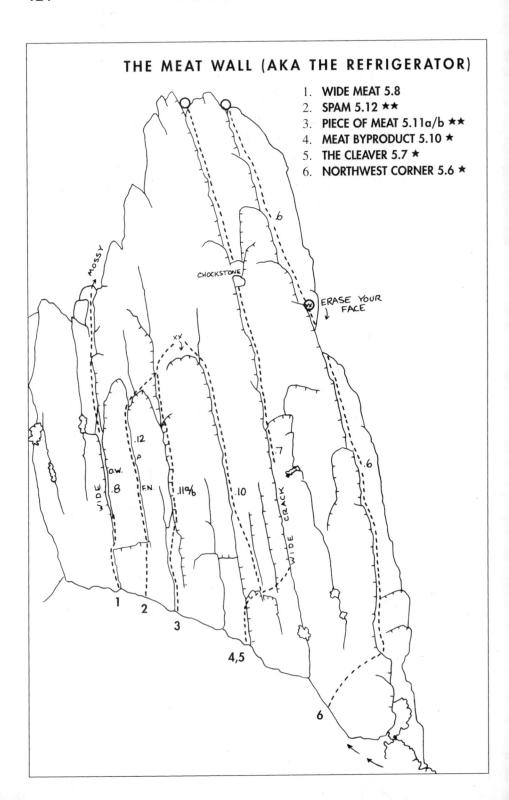

THE MEAT WALL (AKA THE REFRIGERATOR)

1. WIDE MEAT 5.8
2. SPAM 5.12 ★★
3. PIECE OF MEAT 5.11a/b ★★
4. MEAT BYPRODUCT 5.10 ★
5. THE CLEAVER 5.7 ★
6. NORTHWEST CORNER 5.6 ★

## THE MEAT WALL (AKA THE REFRIGERATOR)

**The Meat Wall** is actually the steep north face of the **Green Monster Slab**. It is split by numerous cracks which tend to be smooth and strenuous. The protection is good, the rock is solid, and the routes are in the shade. This is a fine place for a workout.

APPROACH: Approach as for the **Bolt Slab West Face**. At the base of the route **Meadow Muffin**, turn south and scramble up ledges to reach an alcove filled with oak trees. **The Meat Wall** forms the back side of this alcove. See Aerial View page 109.

1. **WIDE MEAT 5.8** A bit wide for most people, it still has redeeming moves.

2. **SPAM 5.12 ★★** Another desperate test piece. This thin crack is witness to many attempts, but few successful leads. The crack overhangs, the footholds are as slippery as spam, and the layaways are off-balance.

3. **PIECE OF MEAT 5.11a/b ★★** A short classic. Good fingerlocks give way to off-hand jamming and a slippery bulge. A definite pump fest.

4. **MEAT BYPRODUCT 5.10 ★** A surprising crack that is harder than it appears. The moves above the start are hard to discern.

5. **THE CLEAVER 5.7 ★** The wide crack that reaches to the top of the cliff. A few pieces of protection in the large size range are helpful.

6. **NORTHWEST CORNER 5.6 ★** Climb the cracks out near the arête. A rounded traverse to the right accesses the crack, and an optional second pitch takes one to the top.

# THE WEST FACES OF GREEN MONSTER SLAB AREA -
## BOLT SLAB, GREEN MONSTER SLAB, AND TINKER TOYS

1. TWO-NUT MUFFIN 5.10a
2. MEADOW MUFFIN 5.12a ★★★
3. ELECTRIC LANDLADY 5.10
4. ERASE YOUR FACE 5.10d ★★
5. GREEN MONSTER AID CRACK 5.10d ★★★
6. GREEN MONSTER 5.9- ★★
7. DIHEDRAL 5.8 ★
8. PURE THOUGHTS 5.11 ★★
9. LEGOS 5.11 ★
10. LINCOLN LOGS 5.9 ★
11. TINKER TOYS 5.7 ★

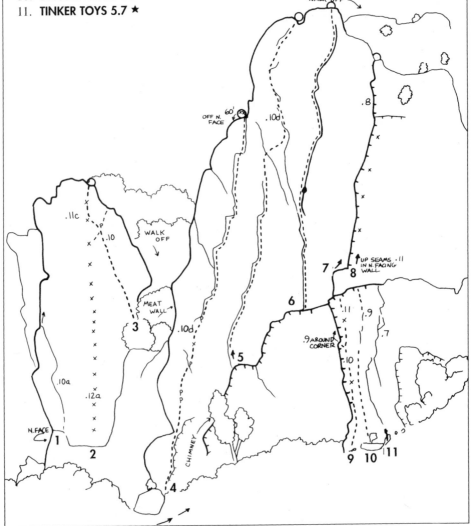

## THE WEST FACES

### BOLT SLAB

Unmistakable because of the sixteen bolt ladder that rises up the center of the west face. The rock is excellent.

1. **TWO-NUT MUFFIN 5.10a** Climb the left side of Bolt Slab, starting in a thin crack and finishing on the arête.

2. **MEADOW MUFFIN 5.12a** ★★★ Somebody's A1 bolt ladder has been transformed into a brilliant thin face test piece. There are more bolts than holds on this route. A traverse to a pin up high is followed by finger locks leftward, to the top. This was likely the first 5.12 in Utah.
   FA: Kim Miller and Mark Ward, 1976.

3. **ELECTRIC LANDLADY 5.10** The right side of **Bolt Slab** presents a fun little route.

### GREEN MONSTER SLAB

The tallest face split by the evident **Green Monster Crack**. One of the best walls in the canyon.

4. **ERASE YOUR FACE 5.10d** ★★ Climb past fixed gear on the left side of the **Green Monster Slab.** Rounded holds abound.

5. **GREEN MONSTER AID CRACK 5.10d** ★★★ A classic. Continuously gnarly climbing up thin cracks in the center of the face. Avoid the **Green Monster** route and the left arête if you want the total effect. Small TCUs and small-to-medium wires.

6. **GREEN MONSTER 5.9** ★★ The apparent hand/fist crack. Bring several friends from 2 to 3-1/2.

7. **DIHEDRAL 5.8** ★ Climb the left-facing dihedral. Many climbers clip the bolts on Pure Thoughts without a second thought.

8. **PURE THOUGHTS 5.11** ★★ Climb the faint seams in the strip of smooth, north-facing rock. Four bolts.

### TINKER TOYS

The next small slab up and south from the **Green Monster Slab**.

9. **LEGOS 5.11** ★ The left arête is either 5.10 or 5.11. Bring small tri-cams.

10. **LINCOLN LOGS 5.9** ★ Climb up to the bolt on **Legos** and continue up thin cracks right of the arête to the top.

11. **TINKER TOYS 5.7** ★ The main crack in the face.

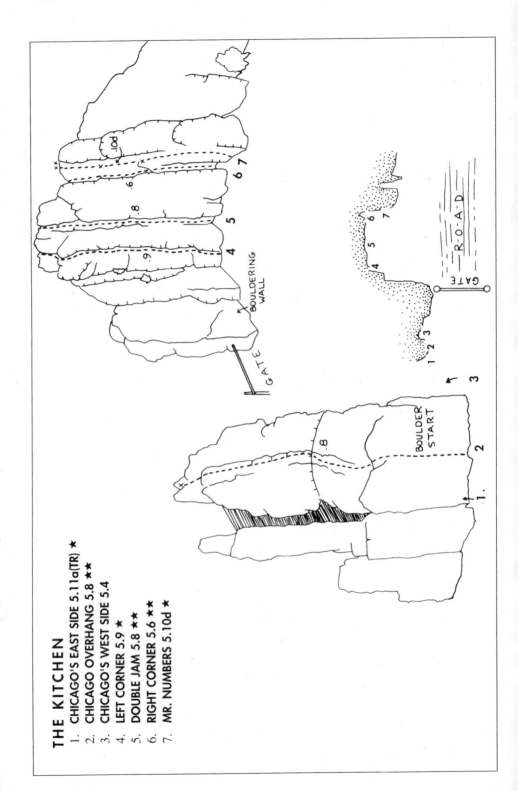

THE KITCHEN

1. CHICAGO'S EAST SIDE 5.11a(TR) ★
2. CHICAGO OVERHANG 5.8 ★★
3. CHICAGO'S WEST SIDE 5.4
4. LEFT CORNER 5.9 ★
5. DOUBLE JAM 5.8 ★★
6. RIGHT CORNER 5.6 ★★
7. MR. NUMBERS 5.10d ★

## THE KITCHEN

**The Kitchen** is one of Rock Canyon's most popular climbing and hang out areas. **The Kitchen** has no approach, steep rock, and can be easily top-roped. The climbs are short, strenuous, and slippery -- expect to find holds with the friction of ice.

APPROACH: Walk or drive up to the gate just past the Waterhouse parking area. At the gate, **The Kitchen** is the immediate wall to the south, and the **Chicago Overhang** is on the next wall up canyon past the gate on the right. See Aerial View page 109.

1. **CHICAGO'S EAST SIDE 5.11a(TR)** ★ A top-rope problem that climbs up the east side of the **Chicago** formation, using face holds and the right edge. If you contrive a line up the face without using the right edge at all, it is 5.12a/b.

2. **CHICAGO OVERHANG 5.8** ★★ The classic Rock Canyon sandbag. A bouldery start is followed by pumper moves out a bulge. The holds are polished and the climbing is hard.

3. **CHICAGO'S WEST SIDE 5.4** Several variations wrestle with the smooth rock on the west face.

4. **LEFT CORNER 5.9** ★ Jam and lieback up the left corner in **The Kitchen.**

5. **DOUBLE JAM 5.8** ★★ The two double cracks vary in size from finger locks to fist jams.

6. **RIGHT CORNER 5.6** ★★ Much easier than it appears.

7. **MR. NUMBERS 5.10d** ★ Climb past two widely spaced bolts, avoiding holds on the **Right Corner** route and on the outside corner. Slippery.

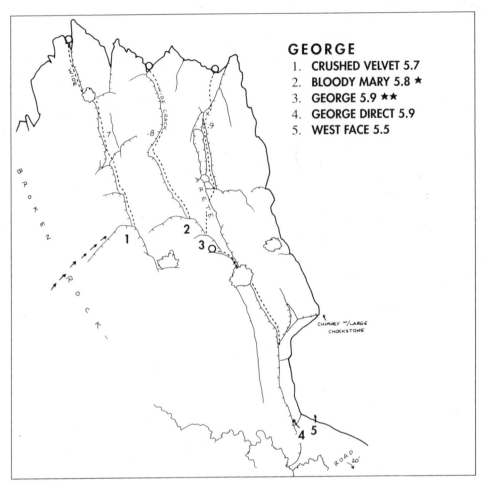

**GEORGE**
1. **CRUSHED VELVET 5.7**
2. **BLOODY MARY 5.8 ★**
3. **GEORGE 5.9 ★★**
4. **GEORGE DIRECT 5.9**
5. **WEST FACE 5.5**

## GEORGE

The **George** wall is the first large wall on the south after the gate and **The Kitchen** area. The rock is more broken here and the routes are less continuous than others in the canyon, with the exception of the route **George**. Most of the routes are exposed and the climbing is good fun. See Aerial View page 109.

1. **CRUSHED VELVET 5.7** The left-most crack system on the wall. Great care should be taken while scrambling to the base.

2. **BLOODY MARY 5.8 ★** This route follows the wide, curving crack in the corner. Strenuous liebacks and wide jams add to the excitement.

3. **GEORGE 5.9 ★★** The best route on the wall. Climb the exposed corner and bulge to the left of the prow. The rock is excellent, the moves are airy, and the adrenaline will flow.

4. **GEORGE DIRECT 5.9** This is the best way to access **George**, as it avoids the scrambling traverse. The rock is loose in places.

5. **WEST FACE 5.5** Several routes can be worked out above the large chockstone.

## THE APPENDAGE

With good rock, and several good climbs, **The Appendage** is a worthy destination. This wall seems private in comparison to **The Kitchen** area, yet the approach takes but a few minutes. Nestled behind some maple trees, these fins of rock face west and south.

APPROACH: 150 feet up canyon from the green gate are two cement retaining walls in the stream. Just up canyon from these wall it is possible to cross the stream to a campsite on the other bank. From the camp follow the left-most trail, which leads up into the oak trees and to **The Appendage,** which sits atop a small talus slope. See Aerial View page 109.

1.  **LEAD 5.7** Climb the west face past a flake and over a wee roof. Clip the last bolt on **The Edge.**

2.  **THE EDGE 5.9** ★ Several good moves on the steep section before going around the corner. Strenuous.
    FA: Darren Knezek.

3.  **ONLY WIMPS TOP ROPE THE BULGE 5.8** You got it. A three bolt jaunt up the west face on fine rock.
    FA: Darren Knezek.

4.  **THE BULGE 5.11b** ★ The prime offering on this wall. Unfortunately, the temptation to stem is very strong on the lower half of the route. However, there is no easy way through the crux.
    FA: Darren Knezek.

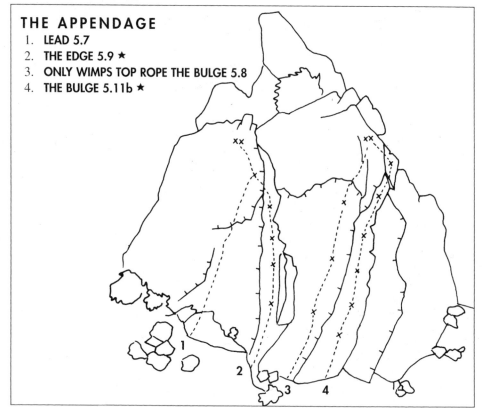

## THE APPENDAGE
1. **LEAD 5.7**
2. **THE EDGE 5.9** ★
3. **ONLY WIMPS TOP ROPE THE BULGE 5.8**
4. **THE BULGE 5.11b** ★

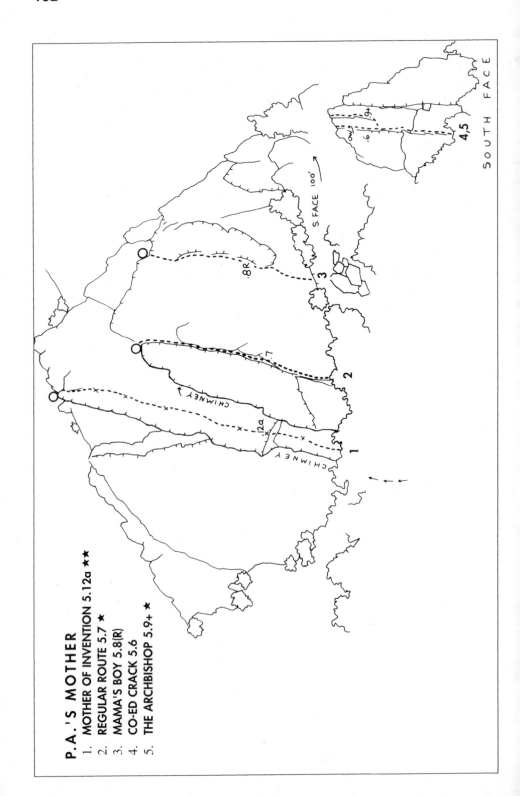

P.A.'S MOTHER
1. MOTHER OF INVENTION 5.12a ★★
2. REGULAR ROUTE 5.7 ★
3. MAMA'S BOY 5.8(R)
4. CO-ED CRACK 5.6
5. THE ARCHBISHOP 5.9+ ★

## P.A.'S MOTHER

**P.A.'s Mother** is less popular than the other walls in the canyon, yet it is host to several quality routes. The rock is solid, the wall is tucked away from "the scene," and the approach is still short.

APPROACH: From the gate at **The Kitchen**, **P.A.'s Mother** can be seen as the west facing wall one hundred yards up canyon on the north side. Walk up the dirt road from the gate, cross the creek bed to reach a talus slope, and scramble up to the base of the routes. See Aerial View page 109.

1. **MOTHER OF INVENTION 5.12a** ★★ Good rock and moves over the lip which are a struggle. Bring some small-medium nuts to protect the sections between bolts.

2. **REGULAR ROUTE 5.7** ★ The obvious wide crack that splits the main wall.

3. **MAMA'S BOY 5.8(R)** A thin route with marginal protection. A bit loose and licheny.

The following two routes are located on a south facing wall one hundred feet up canyon from the **West Face**. It is reached by continuing up the dirt road several hundred feet further than the cutoff to the **West Face**. A short hop across the creek bed reaches the base of the wall.

4. **CO-ED CRACK 5.6** The wide crack that turns into an off-width at the top.

5. **THE ARCHBISHOP 5.9+** ★ Avoid the off-width on **Co-Ed Crack** by traversing right several feet to reach a small crack splitting the headwall. This crack is steeper than it appears. Bring extras in small to medium nuts.

Doug Lee high-stepping **Bosko Loves Barbed Wire [5.10b] Bug Barn Dance Wall**

## ROCK CANYON LIMESTONE

To reach the limestone, simply walk up canyon from the Waterhouse parking area (see page 109) past the green gate which blocks the dirt road at the edge of **The Kitchen,** and continue walking up the road. The fins of quartzite that dominate the lower canyon fade away just after **P.A.'s Mother.** The road winds alongside the stream for another quarter mile through oak trees and cottonwood groves before limestone walls appear on both sides of the canyon. The walk to the first limestone climbing is only ten minutes, but luckily that distance is long enough to keep the crowds down. Take note of the number of stream crossings you encounter, as many of the approaches from the road to the walls are referenced from these crossings.

There are two popular bouldering areas on the limestone. Neither is very extensive, however. The first is a boulder in the stream that sports bolts on top, but can be safely bouldered without a rope by competent climbers. This boulder is located fifty feet down canyon from the signpost, hidden by some trees (see overview map page 136). The second area is the **Eliminator Cave** located at **The Cemetery**. You can crank several steep problems inside of the cave and the landing is good.

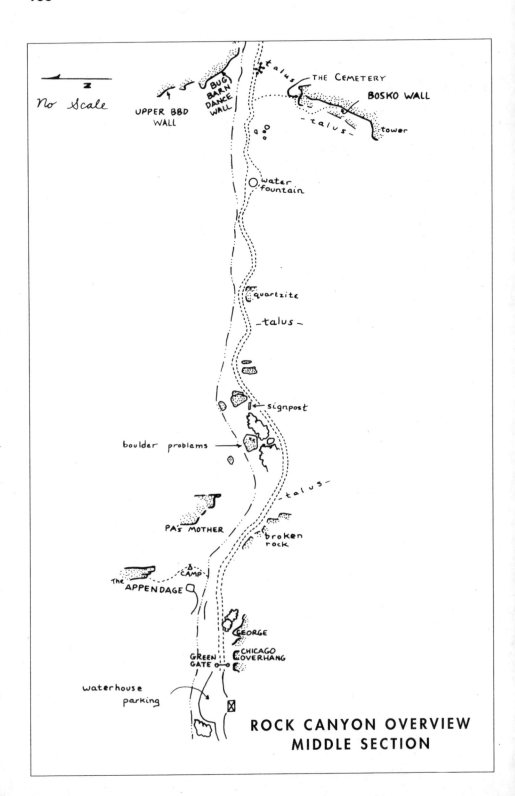

No Scale

UPPER BBD WALL

BUG BARN DANCE WALL

THE CEMETERY

BOSKO WALL

talus

talus

tower

water fountain

quartzite

-talus-

signpost

boulder problems

-talus-

PA's MOTHER

broken rock

CAMP

The APPENDAGE

GEORGE

CHICAGO OVERHANG

GREEN GATE

waterhouse parking

ROCK CANYON OVERVIEW
MIDDLE SECTION

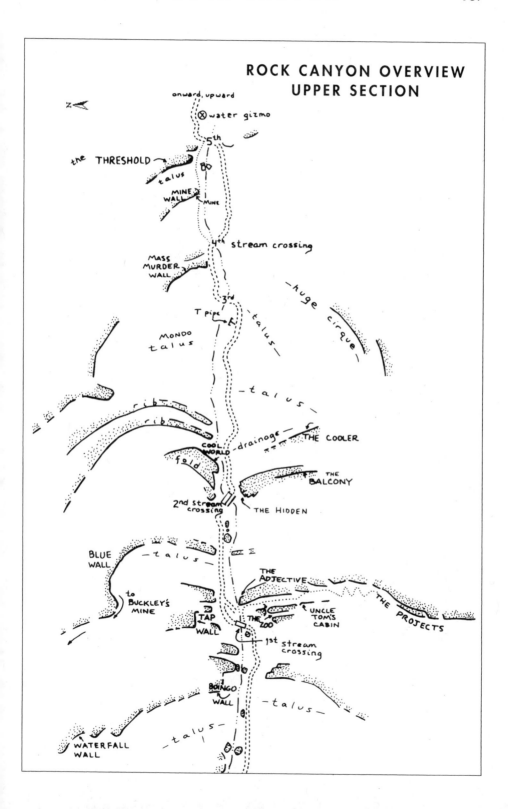

ROCK CANYON OVERVIEW
UPPER SECTION

N

onward, upward

⊗ water gizmo

5th

the THRESHOLD

talus

MINE WALL

MINE

4th stream crossing

MASS MURDER WALL

3rd

huge cirque

T pipe

talus

MONDO talus

talus

rib

rib

talus

drainage

THE COOLER

COOL WORLD

fold

THE BALCONY

2nd stream crossing

THE HIDDEN

BLUE WALL

talus

to BUCKLEY'S MINE

THE ADJECTIVE

THE PROJECTS

TAP WALL

THE ZOO

UNCLE TOM'S CABIN

1st stream crossing

BOINGO WALL

talus

WATERFALL WALL

talus

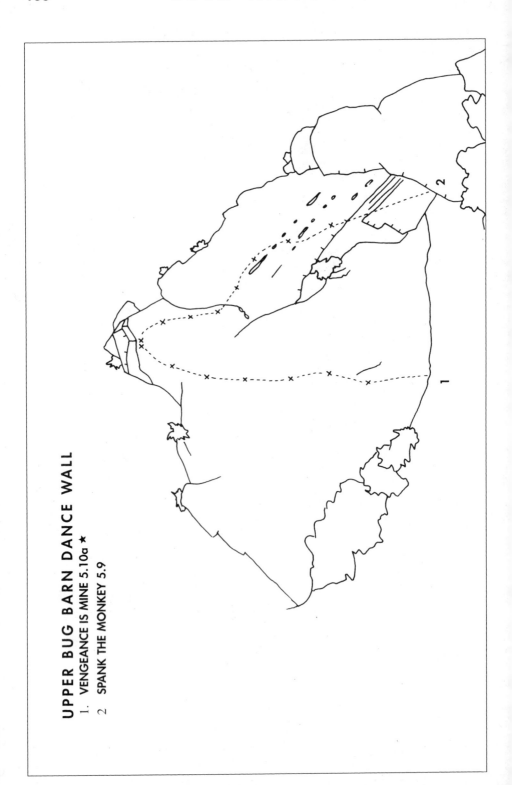

UPPER BUG BARN DANCE WALL
1. VENGEANCE IS MINE 5.10a ★
2 SPANK THE MONKEY 5.9

## DR. TEETH

Located on one of the oddly out-of-place limestone boulders at the very mouth of Rock Canyon. As the name suggests, expect sharp rock. The arête to the left of **Dr. Teeth** can be top-roped off the same anchors.

APPROACH: Several hundred feet before the Turnaround parking area (see page 109), a dirt road meets the main road on the right (south). Park here. Walk west on the dirt road, which turns into a trail. Just before the trail curves to go around the ridge, a steep trail cuts off to the left (south), and heads towards the obvious boulders.

1. **UNKNOWN** An old fixed aid line exists on the front (north side) of the first and lowest boulder.

2. **DR. TEETH 5.10a** Three bolts of technical, balancy climbing up the north face of the upper boulder. Chains at the top. No topo.

## UPPER BUG BARN DANCE WALL

This is a small, separate wall that sits at the upper end of the **Bug Barn Dance Wall** formation. The two routes here face south and cook in the summer heat, but merely sizzle in the spring and fall.

APPROACH: From the upper end of **Bug Barn Dance Wall** (north end), traverse west and cross a small ridge at the notch. Continue traversing west across the talus to the base of the next wall. Follow the base of the wall, climb a small corner, and traverse around the left side. This will put you near the base of **Upper Bug Barn Dance Wall**. See Aerial View page 136.

1. **VENGEANCE IS MINE 5.10a** ★ "Nothing is more costly, nothing is more sterile, than vengeance." -Winston Churchill. Some intricate edge climbing up the center of the face. This route should continue to clean up with more ascents.
   FA: Mark Allman.

2 **SPANK THE MONKEY 5.9** The initial pocket section is good, followed by edges and more slabby climbing.
   FA: Mark Allman.

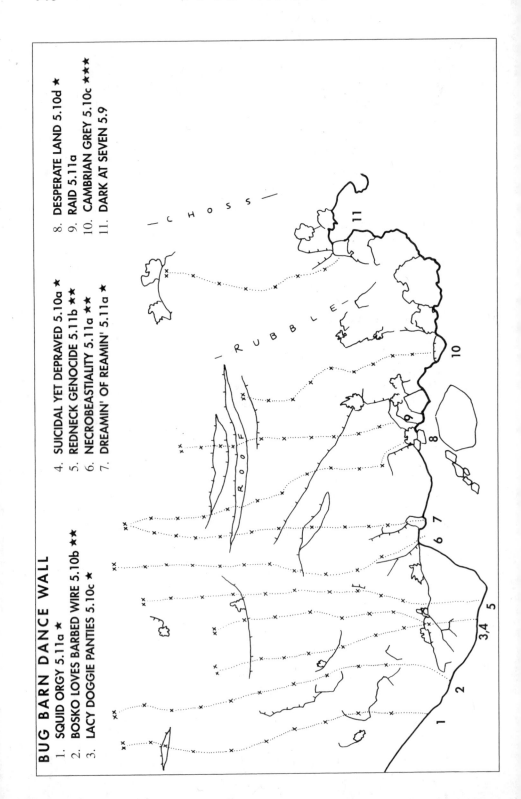

BUG BARN DANCE WALL
1. SQUID ORGY 5.11a ★
2. BOSKO LOVES BARBED WIRE 5.10b ★★
3. LACY DOGGIE PANTIES 5.10c ★

4. SUICIDAL YET DEPRAVED 5.10a ★
5. REDNECK GENOCIDE 5.11b ★★
6. NECROBEASTIALITY 5.11a ★★
7. DREAMIN' OF REAMIN' 5.11a ★

8. DESPERATE LAND 5.10d ★
9. RAID 5.11a
10. CAMBRIAN GREY 5.10c ★★★
11. DARK AT SEVEN 5.9

## BUG BARN DANCE WALL

This wall is the first limestone band to reach the stream. It is also the site of the first limestone route in Rock Canyon. The rock quality is excellent, the climbing requires both power and elegance, and the climbs themselves are memorable as well as enjoyable.

APPROACH: 350 feet up canyon from the water fountain, the first limestone on the left (north) reaches the stream. Cross the stream here, and follow a trail that winds along the base of the cliff. See Aerial View page 136.

1. **SQUID ORGY 5.11a** ★ Good climbing up to a shallow two finger pocket which is the key to turning the roof.
   FA: Phil and Andy Reynolds.

2. **BOSKO LOVES BARBED WIRE 5.10b** ★★ Long, continuous and fun. Crimpy moves on solid edges.
   FA: Phil and Andy Reynolds.

3. **LACY DOGGIE PANTIES 5.10c** ★ The crux is a gaston move, followed by more weirdness.
   FA: Phil and Andy Reynolds.

4. **SUICIDAL YET DEPRAVED 5.10a** ★ "There are many who dare not kill themselves for fear of what the neighbors will say." -Cyril Connolly. Good rock, good edges, good times.
   FA: Phil and Andy Reynolds.

5. **REDNECK GENOCIDE 5.11b** ★★ Very good vertical wall climbing. Positive holds, fun moves, and one wicked crux section. If all else fails, try a full leg press.
   FA: Phil and Andy Reynolds.

6. **NECROBEASTIALITY 5.11a** ★★ High quality. Turn several overhangs on slopers and edges that elicit the beast within.
   FA: Phil and Andy Reynolds.

7. **DREAMIN' OF REAMIN' 5.11a** ★ Roof pulling guaranteed to please.
   FA: Phil Reynolds and Matt Crawley.

8. **DESPERATE LAND 5.10d** ★ Full cruising to a banquet of nothingness.
   FA: Phil Reynolds and Matt Crawley.

9. **RAID 5.11a**
   FA: Mark Allman

10. **CAMBRIAN GREY 5.10c** ★★★ This was the first route established on Rock Canyon limestone. And today, it is still one of the best.
    FA: Chris Laycock.

11. **DARK AT SEVEN 5.9** Eclipsed by the rest of the wall.

## THE CEMETERY

**The Cemetery** is a shaded north facing wall. The rock here is shattered and flaky, not safe for bolt placements, so these routes have been left as top ropes. With so much good climbing available in Rock Canyon, and considering the difficulty of setting up the top ropes, there is little here to recommend. However, the cave to the left of **The Cemetery,** the **Eliminator Cave**, has several good boulder problems, as well as a difficult traverse on the outside edge of the cave.

APPROACH: Walk up canyon 300 feet from the water fountain. A small trail here leads to the right (south). This is 100 feet before a talus slope meets the road, also on the right side. Follow the trail up into the vegetation, moving right to avoid the nasty talus on the left. **The Cemetery** is the northern (lowest) part of the buttress above. To set up the top ropes, approach as for the **Bosko Wall,** then follow the descent listed for the **Bosko Wall.** This will put you at the top of **The Cemetery.** One rappel will reach the top rope anchors, and another will reach the ground. No topo. See Aerial View page 136.

1. **WOODEN KIMONO 5.12a(TR)**
2. **MEMORIAL PARK 5.11d(TR)**
3. **MAUSOLEUM 5.10d(TR)**

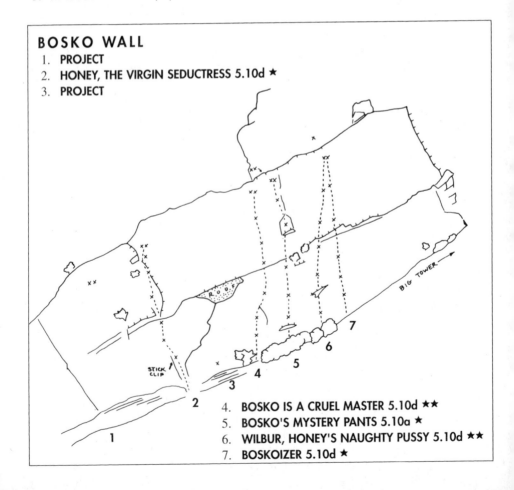

**BOSKO WALL**
1. PROJECT
2. HONEY, THE VIRGIN SEDUCTRESS 5.10d ★
3. PROJECT

4. **BOSKO IS A CRUEL MASTER 5.10d ★★**
5. **BOSKO'S MYSTERY PANTS 5.10a ★**
6. **WILBUR, HONEY'S NAUGHTY PUSSY 5.10d ★★**
7. **BOSKOIZER 5.10d ★**

## BOSKO WALL

This west facing wall is located up high on the south side of the canyon. It involves a tricky approach, and two rappels to get back to the ground. However, the rock is good, the views are quite nice, and crowds won't be a problem.

APPROACH: Walk up canyon 300 feet from the water fountain. A small trail here leads to the right (south). This is 100 feet before a talus slope meets the road on the same side. Follow the trail up into the vegetation, moving right to avoid the nasty talus on the left. This trail leads to **The Cemetery**. From **The Cemetery**, head right, and squeeze between a pine tree and the cliff. Continue up the talus 100 more feet, then start climbing fourth class terrain up and left for 300 feet. Be extremely careful through this section as there is much loose rock. A fall would be disastrous. After the scrambling, skirt up and right another 300 feet along the base of the wall to reach these west facing routes. See Aerial View page 136.

DESCENT: The easiest (and safest) way back down to the ground is to backtrack along the base of the wall, passing where the fourth class section topped out, and continuing down (north) the ledge system, until it ends at a large drop. Two bolts here allow for a rappel which will reach the top of one of **The Cemetery** routes, and one more rappel touches the ground.

1. **PROJECT** Should be good.

2. **HONEY, THE VIRGIN SEDUCTRESS 5.10d ★** Stick clip the first bolt, or get a strong spotter. Boulder the opening moves to reach easier territory above. Some suspect rock on this crack line.
   FA: Phil and Andy Reynolds.

3. **PROJECT**

4. **BOSKO IS A CRUEL MASTER 5.10d ★★** "Weak men are apt to be cruel." -George Savile, Lord Halifax. The cranking moves at the crux are cruel to master.
   FA: Phil and Andy Reynolds.

5. **BOSKO'S MYSTERY PANTS 5.10a ★** Climb up the more broken corner system, which provides many rests and a few good moves.
   FA: Phil and Andy Reynolds.

6. **WILBUR, HONEY'S NAUGHTY PUSSY 5.10d ★★** Interesting throughout. Turn two small roofs on edges and good rock.
   FA: Phil and Andy Reynolds.

7. **BOSKOIZER 5.10d ★** More of the same: edges, good stone, a roof.
   FA: Phil and Andy Reynolds.

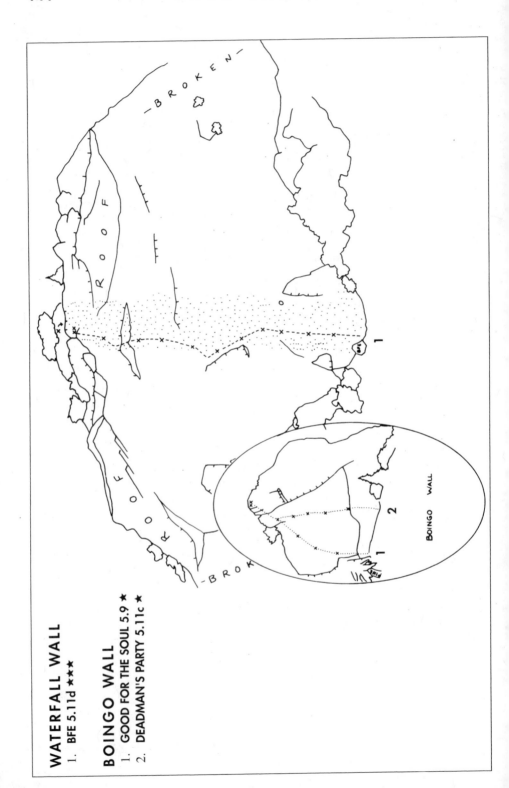

WATERFALL WALL
1. BFE 5.11d ★★★

BOINGO WALL
1. GOOD FOR THE SOUL 5.9 ★
2. DEADMAN'S PARTY 5.11c ★

## WATERFALL WALL

This lone wall sits high on the north side of the canyon. The one route here is a classic, and climbs directly up a blue water streak that is prominent from as far away as the mouth of the canyon. Some potential exists here for other routes, but the best features of this wall are the solitude and the views. This route will likely be wet in spring or after big storms. A word of caution, however. The **Waterfall Wall** sits in the direct path of any rocks knocked down by hikers from above on the **Buckley's Mine** trail. Be extremely careful if there are hikers around (especially on weekends), or if you use the second approach listed below. See Aerial View page 137.

APPROACH: There are two options for reaching this wall. The first way described is more direct, and perhaps easier going up, but more difficult on the way down. For this approach, walk up canyon 150 feet past the **Bug Barn Dance Wall** to a spot where you can reach the talus gully coming in from the left (north). Hike up this gully to a fourth class slab section which can be climbed on its left (southwest) side. Continue veering left, and round the small cliff band on the left (west) side. Walk in a northwest direction, across some talus, and go up the second gully on the right (northeast). Thrash directly through the brush to reach the base of the route.

This second option takes longer, but the walk down is fairly easy. Great care must be taken because of rockfall on this approach. Hike up to the **Blue Wall** area, along the **Buckley's Mine** trail. About eight minutes past the **Blue Wall,** heading towards **Buckley's Mine,** is an overlook (a diving board vista point). Continue walking west on the trail and carefully head down the second gully on the left (south) past the vista point. This gully leads to the top of the waterfall, where one rappel off a bolt and a tree take you down to the base. Be careful when you pull down your rope, as rocks will likely follow.

1. **BFE 5.11d ★★★** A real gem. Beautiful, technical climbing up the left side of the water streak. The moves near the top require both power and finesse. The bolts on this route are exposed to a lot of water. In two years they have shown marked deterioration. Chem-bolts should be considered as a replacement.
   FA: Darren Knezek.

## BOINGO WALL

This is a steep west facing wall with two tricky routes. Both routes are packed with hard moves and good engaging climbing.

APPROACH: Walk up the road 300 feet past the **Bug Barn Dance Wall** to a largish limestone stone boulder with an almost flat top. Cross the stream, walk right (east) on a culvert for 50 feet, and then follow the trail 200 feet up the scree and into the trees at the base of the wall. See Aerial View page 137.

1. **GOOD FOR THE SOUL 5.9 ★** Awkward and slopey holds that indulge the psyche.
   FA: Robert Kleinman.

2. **DEADMAN'S PARTY 5.11c ★** Hard sequences that climb like a bolted boulder problem. Many leaders think that the crux is clipping the third bolt.
   FA: Robert Kleinman.

# UNCLE TOM'S CABIN
1. C'EST COOL 5.12a ★★

# THE ZOO
1. CALDER'S ROUTE 5.8
2. LIGHTNING BOLT 5.11b/c ★
3. EXCESSIVE BAIL 5.11a ★★
4. THE ZOO 5.10b ★

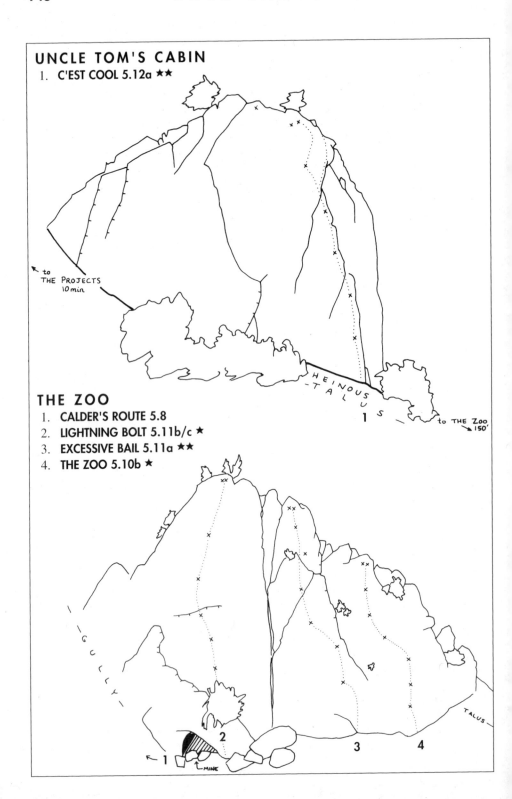

## UNCLE TOM'S CABIN

There is one route located on this fin of east facing limestone, and room for two more desperates. The rock is bullet hard, but the base of the wall is an awful mixture of loose, steep talus.

APPROACH: Instead of crossing the bridge at the first stream crossing, continue along the right (south) bank of the stream for 100 feet. Turn right (south) and walk up the gully for 350 feet, passing the notch that leads to the zoo and passing the remnants of an old mining shack. See Aerial View page 137.

1. **C'EST COOL 5.12a ★★** Allez, Allez! A tricky crack that involves flared jams and thin moves. That combo is followed by one "stopper" move going left, or more reasonable crack climbing going right.
   FA: Steve Bullock.

## THE ZOO

This is a fine wall with a cage-full of good routes. The rock is solid, and when pockets appear, they are usually really good. The routes are steeper than they look, or at least feel steeper and more pumpy than would be expected for this vertical, east facing wall. In the summer, this is a nice afternoon destination.

APPROACH: Instead of crossing the bridge at the first stream crossing, continue along the right bank of the stream for 100 feet. Turn right (south) and walk up the gully for 200 feet until a notch appears on the right (west). Walk through this notch and voile'. See Aerial View page 137.

1. **CALDER'S ROUTE 5.8** A two bolt route up the wall to the left of the mine entrance.
   FA: Calder Stratford.

2. **LIGHTNING BOLT 5.11b/c ★** Small finger edges on a technical, pumpy face that will shock the malaise right out of you.
   FA: Bill Ohran.

3. **EXCESSIVE BAIL 5.11a ★★** Really good climbing that doesn't ease up where you think it might. Good pockets and many sidepulls that are costly on the arms.
   FA: Glen Oross.

4. **THE ZOO 5.10b ★** "The city is not a concrete jungle. It is a human zoo." Desmond Morris. A great opening pocket sequence gets things rolling. From there, continue up and left on slopers, sidepulls, and good pockets.
   FA: Tom Caldwell.

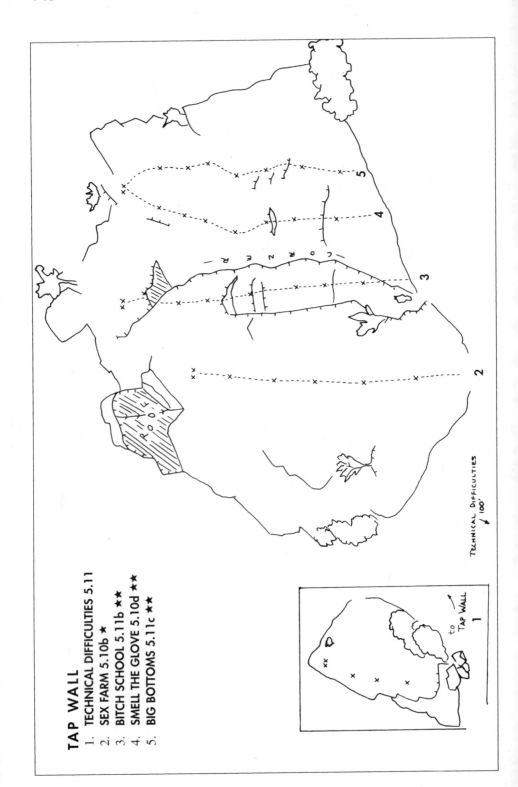

TAP WALL
1. TECHNICAL DIFFICULTIES 5.11
2. SEX FARM 5.10b ★
3. BITCH SCHOOL 5.11b ★★
4. SMELL THE GLOVE 5.10d ★★
5. BIG BOTTOMS 5.11c ★★

## TAP WALL

This deceptively steep, south facing wall is partially hidden by trees. The climbing here is characterized by good edges, bulges, and solid rock.

APPROACH: Make the first stream crossing at the bridge. Stop and look north. **Technical Difficulties** is an east-facing wall 30 feet from the road. Tap wall is 100 feet up the scree to the north of **Technical Difficulties**. The huge roof on the **Tap Wall** is visible from the stream crossing. See Aerial View page 137.

1.  **TECHNICAL DIFFICULTIES 5.11** Getting nothing but static. A short route that is bouldery and dirty.
    FA: Phil Reynolds.

2.  **SEX FARM 5.10b ★** Plough up good edges on good rock. Not as steep as the other routes on this wall.
    FA: Mark Allman and Steve Alison.

3.  **BITCH SCHOOL 5.11b ★★** Quite an education. Try to do this route without stemming. The roofs up high round out the experience.
    FA: Mark Allman.

4.  **SMELL THE GLOVE 5.10d ★★** A fine excursion up this steep wall, with bulge after bulge of indulgence.
    FA: Mark Allman and Steve Alison.

5.  **BIG BOTTOMS 5.11c ★★** "A big man has no time really to do anything but just sit and be big." -F. Scott Fitzgerald. Treat yourself to bulging forearms by turning multiple bulges on small, less obvious edges.
    FA: Mark Allman.

Jeff Pedersen demonstrating his mastery of **Valhalla [5.13b/c] The Projects**

## THE PROJECTS

This is the best wall in Rock Canyon for steep, hard routes. The rock is solid and beautiful, and the wall stays shady until late afternoon. The climbing is characterized by powerful, often bouldery sequences, intricate footwork, and the occasional desperate slab finish. In other words, these routes reflect first ascensionist Jeff Pedersen's penchant for combining power with aesthetics. Several of the regions top ten hardest routes are found at **The Projects.** Although there is a high concentration of difficult routes here, the crowds prefer the short approach of the **Hell** area and a day spent working on a route at **The Projects** is often a pleasantly lonely experience. Several routes require a sixty meter rope to lower off. These will be noted in the individual route descriptions.

APPROACH: Instead of crossing the bridge at the first stream crossing, continue along the right (south) bank of the stream for 100 feet. Turn right (south) and head up the gully passing the notch that leads to The Zoo, and another 150 feet higher, passing **Uncle Tom's Cabin**. Struggle for another 200 feet up bad, loose talus. From this point, the walking becomes progressively easier. Continue up the gully until **The Projects** appear on the left (east), about 15 minutes from the stream crossing. See Aerial View page 137.

1.  **STILLETTO 5.11c** ★★ A thinking person's route. Technical, footwork intensive, and first rate.
    FA: Mark Allman.

2.  **BLANKET PARTY 5.12a** ★ A boulder problem followed by weirdness. The bouldery moves are on slopy crimps.
    FA: Jeff Pederson.

3.  **DROGEN 5.12c** ★★ Means drugs in Swedish. Technical climbing down low, bouldery climbing up high and a rest in between.
    FA: Bill Ohran.

4.  **F.AWAY 5.12b** ★★ Not for the impotent. Approach-type climbing leads to a string of hard moves with good value.
    FA: Jeff Pedersen.

5.  **WATCH YOUR FACE 5.13c/d** ★★ Continuously difficult pulling to a heartbreaker slab finish.
    FA: Jeff Pedersen.

6.  **PROJECT**

7.  **JUNKIE PRIDE 5.13b** ★★★ Wicked continuous, with good pulls and bad feet. Tres bon!
    FA: Bill Ohran.

8.  **JUNKIE BITCH 5.13b** ★★ A variation. Climb to the sixth bolt on **Junkie Pride**, and cut left to join the top of route number 6.
    FA: Bill Ohran.

9.  **PROJECT**

10. **HEY WHITEY 5.13d** ★★★ A JPU diploma is required for a successful ascent of this desperate. Use a wild combination of bear hugs, slaps, and dihedral/arête climbing.
    FA: Jeff Pedersen.

11. **DEAD DEVIL 5.12d ★★** A 60 meter rope is needed. Technical for the grade with a reach dependent crux.
FA: Jeff Pedersen.

12. **PROJECT** A conceived line cutting off to the right near the top of **Dead Devil**.

13. **DRAIN 5.12b ★★** Long, thin and pumpy. This route has the potential to make good climbers look bad. This was the first redpointed route at **The Projects.** A 60 meter rope will reach the ground, or you can use the station halfway down the route.
FA: Darren Knezek, Matt Nielson.

14. **MUTILATION 5.11b ★★** The popular warm up route. Good movement. A 60 meter rope is needed, or use the bolt station halfway down the route.
FA: Darren Knezek.

15. **LURCH 5.12c ★** While standing on the ledge most climbers pull their rope up through the first four bolts to prevent rope drag. Heinous slab moves at the top complete this wild ride.
FA: Darren Knezek.

16. **VALHALLA 5.13b/c ★★★** Impeccable rock. A classic that bestows a bouldery start, several gaston moves, a roof, and a slab move requiring a windshield wiper sweep with the right arm.
FA: Jeff Pedersen.

17. **MR. CONCRETE 5.13b ★★** It's severe, but persevere. High quality for a short package.
FA: Jeff Pedersen.

18. **PROJECT** "Bill Ohran's pipe dream."

19. **SLUMLORD 5.12d ★★** The rent is due. Killer. Power and endurance.
FA: Jeff Pedersen.

20. **THE BILLYCLUB (PROJECT)**

21. **FISHWIFE 5.11a ★** The bush near the top is off limits! A good introduction to steep climbing that resembles a poor person's version of the route **Hell.**
FA: Darren Knezek.

22. **PROJECT**

23. **GUTTERBOY 5.13a ★★** Bouldery, with several slaps and six consecutive moves of bad holds.
FA: Jeff Pedersen.

24. **CURBJOB 5.12c ★★** An optimum route that can disappoint if you're bouldering skills aren't honed. Very nice rock.
FA: Jeff Pedersen.

25. **LADIES FIRST (VARIATION) 5.12b ★** Climb **Curbjob** for three bolts, then move right and up past two bolts to join Inferior at its third bolt.
FA: Darren Greenhall.

26. **INFERIOR 5.11b ★★** An inferior name because of its diminutive numbers.
FA: Jeff Pedersen.

27. **APPROACH ROUTE A0** or **5.8** Four bolts that can be clipped, pulled up on, and used as footholds if needed. This is the access route to the ledge and the cave above. Leave the quickdraws hanging for the day to make climbing up and back down

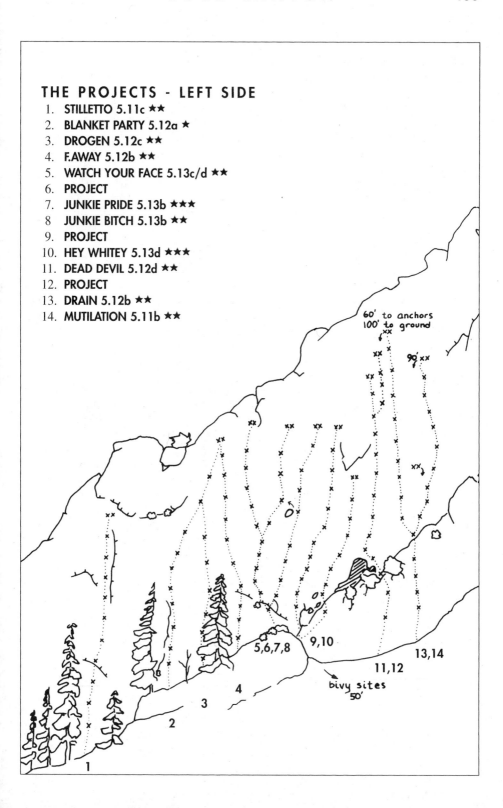

## THE PROJECTS - LEFT SIDE
1. STILLETTO 5.11c ★★
2. BLANKET PARTY 5.12a ★
3. DROGEN 5.12c ★★
4. F.AWAY 5.12b ★★
5. WATCH YOUR FACE 5.13c/d ★★
6. PROJECT
7. JUNKIE PRIDE 5.13b ★★★
8 JUNKIE BITCH 5.13b ★★
9. PROJECT
10. HEY WHITEY 5.13d ★★★
11. DEAD DEVIL 5.12d ★★
12. PROJECT
13. DRAIN 5.12b ★★
14. MUTILATION 5.11b ★★

60' to anchors
100' to ground

90' xx

5,6,7,8

9,10

13,14

11,12

bivy sites
50'

4

3

2

1

**THE PROJECTS - RIGHT SIDE**
15. **LURCH 5.12c ★**
16. **VALHALLA 5.13b/c ★★★**
17. **MR. CONCRETE 5.13b ★★**
18. **PROJECT**
19. **SLUMLORD 5.12d ★★**
20. **THE BILLYCLUB (PROJECT)**
21. **FISHWIFE 5.11a ★**
22. **PROJECT**

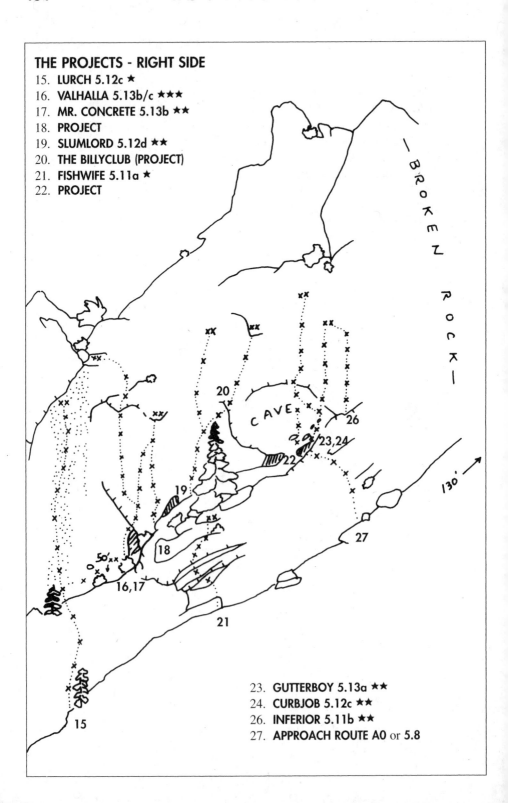

23. **GUTTERBOY 5.13a ★★**
24. **CURBJOB 5.12c ★★**
26. **INFERIOR 5.11b ★★**
27. **APPROACH ROUTE A0** or **5.8**

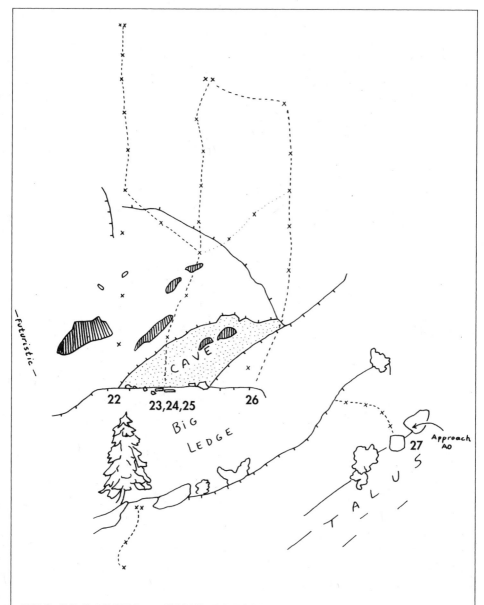

## THE PROJECTS - CAVE DETAIL
22. **PROJECT**
23. **GUTTERBOY 5.13a ★★**
24. **CURBJOB 5.12c ★★**
25. **LADIES FIRST (VARIATION) 5.12b ★**
26. **INFERIOR 5.11b ★★**
27. **APPROACH ROUTE A0** or **5.8**

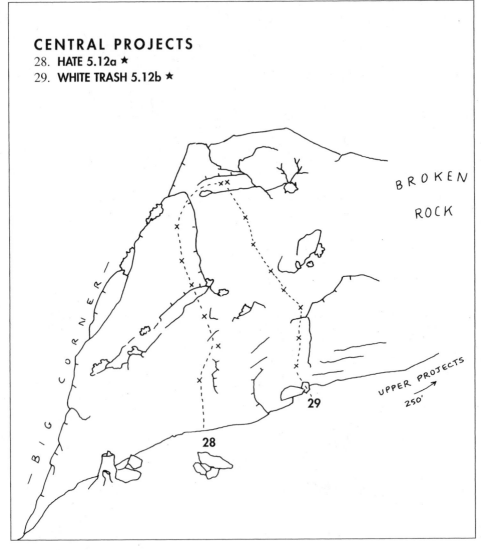

**CENTRAL PROJECTS**
28. **HATE 5.12a** ★
29. **WHITE TRASH 5.12b** ★

BROKEN

ROCK

BIG CORNER

UPPER PROJECTS
250'

29

28

## CENTRAL PROJECTS

Steep and pumpy rock, with two routes and finally, a flat base.

APPROACH: Continue walking up hill past **The Projects** for 130 feet. These two routes sit above a more pleasant flat spot in the pines. See Aerial View page 137.

28. **HATE 5.12a** ★ "I never hated a man enough to give him his diamonds back." -Zsa Zsa Gabor. An ensemble of steep rock and pumpy moves.
    FA: Jeremy Brown.

29. **WHITE TRASH 5.12b** ★ A boulder problem at the start wastes many climbers. Once that move is disposed, enjoy the easier climbing above.
    FA: Bill Ohran.

## UPPER PROJECTS

A beautiful wall worth the extra hike uphill from **The Projects.** Potential exists here for more steep hard routes.

APPROACH: Continue walking up hill past **The Projects** for 380 feet. You'll pass the **Central Projects** at a flat spot in the pines, and then join a talus slope. The **Upper Projects** are to the left (east) of this talus. Look for the prominent grey/blue streak. See Aerial View page 137.

30. **WHITE LINE 5.10a** ★ Snort up this line of edges on less than vertical rock.
    FA: Calder Stratford.

31. **SPOONS AND NEEDLES 5.12a** ★★ A prime offering of steep rock, edges, and addictive moves.
    FA: Bill Ohran.

32. **TRACKS 5.11b/c** ★★ All the makings of quintessence: crimpers, good rock, a bulge.
    FA: Bill Ohran.

33. **CRACK 5.10c** Self explanatory.
    FA: Bill Ohran.

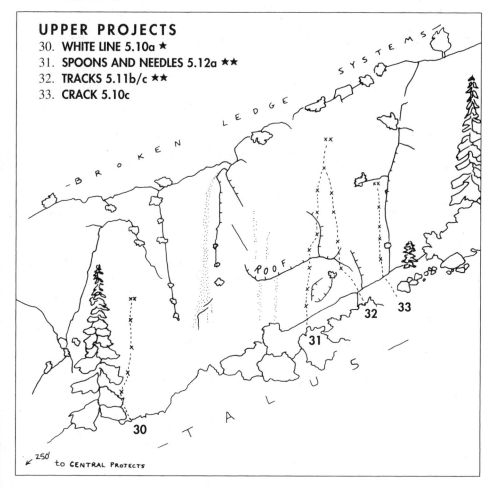

**UPPER PROJECTS**
30. **WHITE LINE 5.10a** ★
31. **SPOONS AND NEEDLES 5.12a** ★★
32. **TRACKS 5.11b/c** ★★
33. **CRACK 5.10c**

## WEST SIDE WALL

A small cliff with good rock and one good route.

APPROACH: Approach as for **The Projects.** 100 feet to the right (west) of the routes **Hey Whitey**, and **Drain**, are several level bivy sites near the edge of the ridge. Hike up the slab 20 feet above the bivy sites, then follow a ramp down and west via some fourth class climbing to reach the base of this wall. No topo.

1.  **UNKNOWN**
2.  **SPANK 5.11d ★** A micro-classic. An accuracy problem to a tiny handhold.
    FA: Bill Ohran.


## THE ADJECTIVE

Tucked among a grove of trees and close to the stream, **The Adjective** is a perfect summer wall. The climbing is characterized by impeccable rock, square edges, and corner systems or striking arêtes. Climbing here is a first-rate experience.

APPROACH: Walk 100 feet further up canyon from the first stream crossing. Turn right (south) towards the stream and the wall that the stream runs along. Cross the stream at the left (east) edge of that wall and wander 30 feet trough the trees to this east facing wall. See Aerial View page 137.

1.  **PROJECT**
2.  **FURIOUS 5.11c ★** "No man can think clearly when his fists are clenched." George Jean Nathan. A dry heaves version of **Vomit.** Hard moves and harder holds may leave you seething.
    FA: Darren Knezek.
3.  **VOMIT 5.10d ★** Jug illusions. All those big edges that turn out to be sloping are cause for a malox moment, but the final eruption occurs while attempting to clip the chains.
    FA: Darren Knezek.
4.  **FEROCIOUS 5.12b ★★** It is easy to deviate to the sides of the intended line, but regardless, the climbing is brilliant and packed with savage moves.
    FA: Danny Kohlert.
5.  **PROJECT**
6.  **PINK BICYCLE (PROJECT)** climbs corner.
7.  **ATROCIOUS 5.11c ★** A beautiful arête that is marred by the proximity of easy climbing just around the corner. Do this route anyhow, it still has hard moves and fun climbing.
    FA: Danny Kohlert.

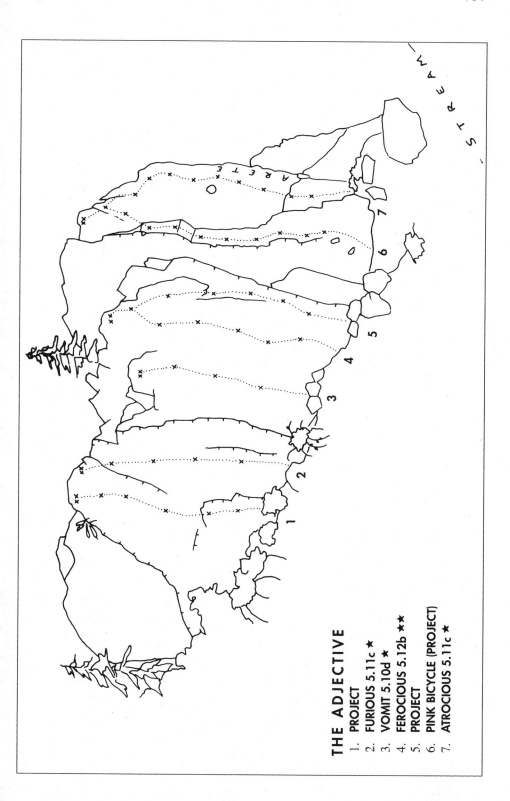

THE ADJECTIVE
1. PROJECT
2. FURIOUS 5.11c ★
3. VOMIT 5.10d ★
4. FEROCIOUS 5.12b ★★
5. PROJECT
6. PINK BICYCLE (PROJECT)
7. ATROCIOUS 5.11c ★

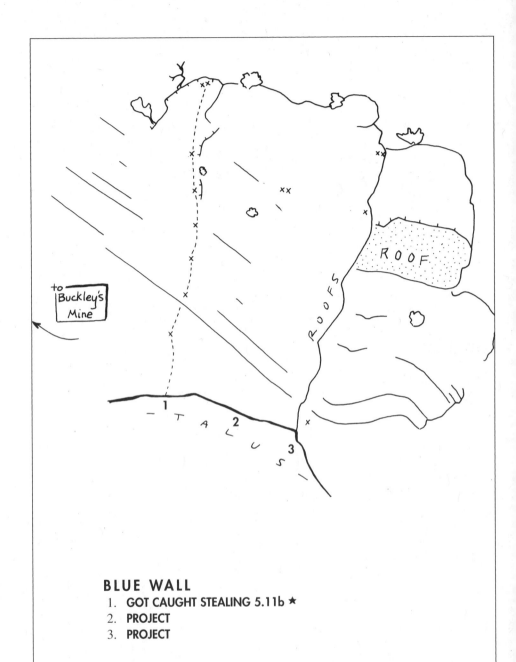

**BLUE WALL**
1.  GOT CAUGHT STEALING 5.11b ★
2.  PROJECT
3.  PROJECT

## BLUE WALL

Pulling on diagonal striations, and feeling off balance is the nature of the climbing at the **Blue Wall.** South facing, this wall soaks up fall sun but is apparently shaded in winter. Expect a pump--the routes are steeper than they appear.

APPROACH: 250 feet up canyon from the first stream crossing and 100 feet down canyon from the second stream crossing is a talus slope on the left (north). Walk up this talus, passing the prominent blue streaks on the wall to the right (east). Continue for another 200 feet to a point where the wall bends from running north and south to running east and west. The routes are to the left (west) of the big roof, and face south. This approach is the start of the popular **Buckley's Mine** trail. See Aerial View page 137.

1. **GOT CAUGHT STEALING 5.11b** ★ A fun route that is both technical and powerful. Although a bit scary getting to the first bolt, the balancy climbing through the roofs make this jaunt worthwhile. The glued hold at the fourth bolt should be treated gingerly.
   FA: John Walter.

2. **PROJECT**

3. **PROJECT**

## BUCKLEY'S MINE WALL

A steep wall with one route and a popular mine shaft to explore after the climbing is finished.

APPROACH: Approach as for the **Blue Wall,** but continue hiking west for another fifteen minutes along a surprisingly good trail that contours in and out of several gullies. The views of the city are awesome from here, and are worth the hike alone. This wall faces south and can be almost as pleasant on sunny winter days as during spring and fall. Potential exists for more routes in this area. See Aerial View page 137.

1. **WE'RE NOT IN KANSAS ANYMORE 5.11b** ★ Start ten feet right of the mine and climb past five bolts along a blue streak. A stem in the middle marks the crux. No topo.
   FA: Tom Caldwell.

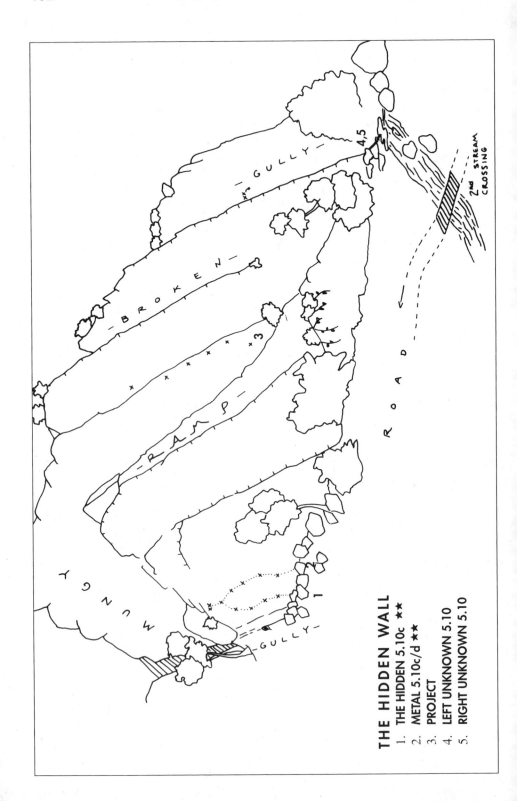

**THE HIDDEN WALL**
1. THE HIDDEN 5.10c ★★
2. METAL 5.10c/d ★★
3. PROJECT
4. LEFT UNKNOWN 5.10
5. RIGHT UNKNOWN 5.10

## THE HIDDEN WALL

**The Hidden Wall** is actually the northern terminus of **The Balcony.** The climbs here face either north or west and stay cool even on the hottest days. Much of the upper part of this buttress is shattered rock, but the following routes make good use of the lower, high quality stone.

APPROACH: When you reach the bridge at the second stream crossing, stop. Directly in front of you is a steep wall with a prominent left-leaning crack facing the road. This is **The Hidden** wall. Route number three is the crack, and routes four and five are located on a small, slabby west-facing wall just down canyon and around the corner from the crack. See Aerial View page 137.

1. **THE HIDDEN 5.10c** ★★ Slopey holds interspersed with positive edges on good solid rock.
   FA: Darren Knezek.

2. **METAL 5.10c/d** ★★ Underclings and liebacks ensure undiluted fun.
   FA: Darren Knezek.

3. **PROJECT** The half bolted, left leaning, thin crack that faces the road.
   FA: In progress, Bill Ohran.

4. **LEFT UNKNOWN 5.10** Several thin crack moves at the start require a mixture of good footwork and good balance. Short, with three bolts.

5. **RIGHT UNKNOWN 5.10** Although it looks like you could just march up the corner to the right, closer inspection of that option will reveal that it is a no go. A hard stem starts things off, followed by a few thin cranks. Very short on very smooth rock.

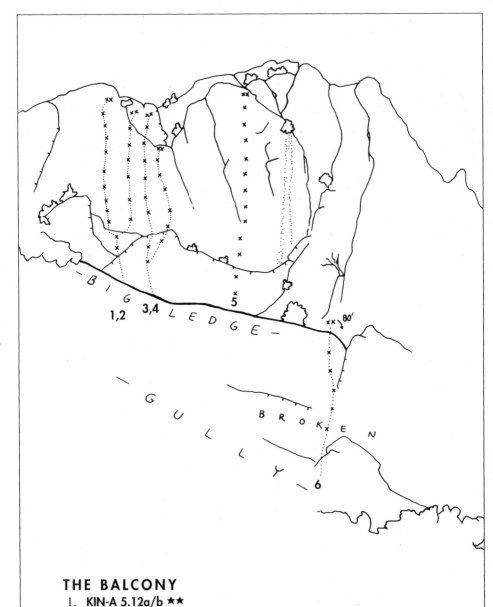

## THE BALCONY

1. KIN-A 5.12a/b ★★
2. SLACKER 5.12a ★★★
3. LEARNING TO FLY 5.11d ★★★
4. SNAKEJUICE 5.11c ★
5. PROJECT
6. APPROACH PITCH 5.9(R)

## THE BALCONY

One of the finest walls in the canyon. Don't let the approach pitch put you off, the steep climbing, solid rock and grand views more than make up for the hassle.

APPROACH: Walk 150 feet up canyon from the second stream crossing. Turn right (south) at a small trail that heads towards the east face of the large wall you just walked past. Follow this trail as it enters the gully, thrash through a little brush, and continue following the gully to the base of the approach pitch which is on the right (west) wall. See Aerial View page 137.

1. **KIN-A 5.12a/b ★★** A field day for the vice-grip family. High quality pinching and pulling. Long and demanding.
   FA: Darren Knezek.

2. **SLACKER 5.12a ★★★** A constant hunt for holds. Excellent thin edge climbing with a head spinning exit move.
   FA: Bill Ohran.

3. **LEARNING TO FLY 5.11d ★★★** One of the canyon's best. Continuous face climbing on good edges up impeccable limestone.
   FA: Bill Ohran.

4. **SNAKEJUICE 5.11c ★** More of the same marvelous stuff, only shorter and a bit sharper than the other routes.
   FA: Matt Nielson.

5. **PROJECT** A mega route in the making.
   FA: Bill Ohran.

6. **APPROACH PITCH 5.9(R)** Five bolts lead up a broken corner system to access the large ledge at the base of the main wall. The anchors at the top of this pitch allow for an 80 foot rappel back into the gully.

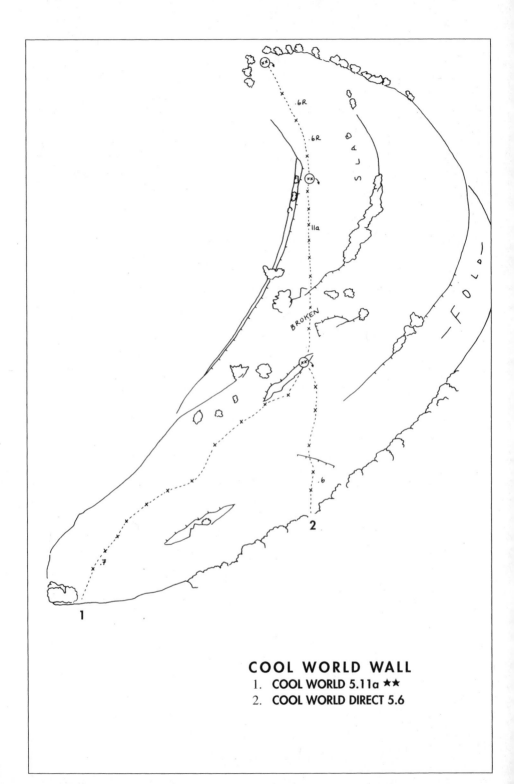

**COOL WORLD WALL**
1. COOL WORLD 5.11a ★★
2. COOL WORLD DIRECT 5.6

## COOL WORLD WALL

Two routes reside on the east face of this huge fold of rock. Both make good use of the silica deposits within the limestone for hand and foot holds. The route **Cool World** follows a winding line of good rock up the spine of the buttress and concludes with a rewarding view at the end of three pitches.

APPROACH: Walk up canyon 200 feet from the second stream crossing. On the left (north) is a major fold of rock, which drops down to the stream. The following two routes are located on the east (up canyon) face of this wall. From the road walk twenty five feet down to the stream, cross the stream, and you will be at the base of the climbs. See Aerial View page 137.

1. **COOL WORLD 5.11a ★★** Three pitches. Wear those comfy shoes or this could be a cruel world. The first pitch climbs on brown swirlygigs up and right to a two bolt belay/rappel anchor. (11 bolts). The second pitch requires great care while climbing through the broken rock above the belay. This brings you to the steep face above, which seems to be easier to the left of the bolt line. The belay/rappel station is right where the angle of the rock begins to relent. (8 bolts). On the last pitch, climb on the cool brown plates past three widely spaced bolts to a rappel anchor. Three rappels from the top reach the ground. There is a high probability of getting a rope stuck on the first two rappels.
   FA: Darren Knezek.

2. **COOL WORLD DIRECT 5.6** A direct start to the first pitch of **Cool World** that crosses many ledges and blocks.
   FA: Darren Knezek.

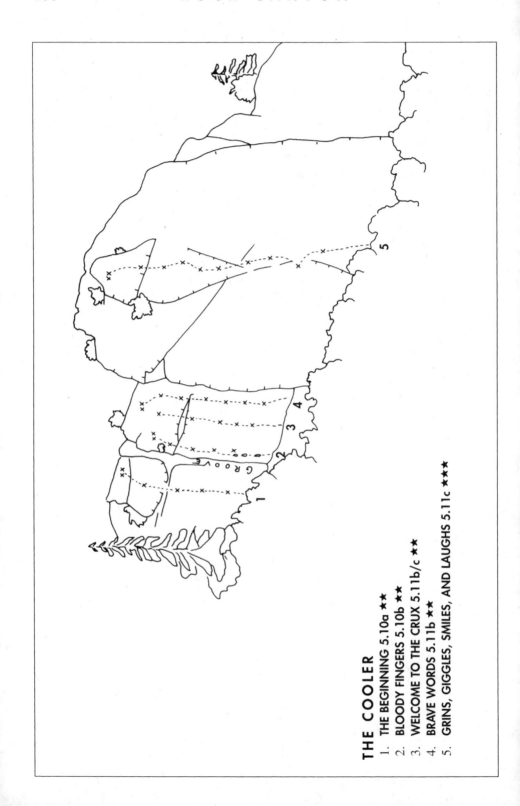

THE COOLER
1. THE BEGINNING 5.10a ★★
2. BLOODY FINGERS 5.10b ★★
3. WELCOME TO THE CRUX 5.11b/c ★★
4. BRAVE WORDS 5.11b ★★
5. GRINS, GIGGLES, SMILES, AND LAUGHS 5.11c ★★★

## THE COOLER

The cooler is an east facing wall with numerous quality climbs. The rock here is vertical, littered with edges and tiny features. The routes are sustained, intricate, balancy, and very good. Some of the edges are surprisingly sharp.

APPROACH: Walk 250 feet up canyon from the second stream crossing. A drainage on the right (south) comes down from a huge cirque and meets the road. Walk up this drainage, staying close to the small cliff band on the right (west). This wall leads directly to **The Cooler.** If the water is too high to walk in the streambed, follow the left hand branch of the drainage until it is possible to cut through the brush directly to the highest part of the wall, which is **The Cooler.** See Aerial View page 137.

1. **THE BEGINNING 5.10a ★★** Let there be positive, sharp, finger edges up a line without a distinct crux.
   FA: Bill Ohran.

2. **BLOODY FINGERS 5.10b ★★** Stay left of the initial bolts, working the big pockets, then move back to the crimpers.
   FA: Bill Ohran.

3. **WELCOME TO THE CRUX 5.11b/c ★★** Excellent climbing leads to a high, balancy clip; followed by a micro thin, height-dependent crux.
   FA: Bill Ohran.

4. **BRAVE WORDS 5.11b ★★** An overhanging start limbers up the fingers for some stoic reaches on the face above.
   FA: Bill Ohran.

5. **GRINS, GIGGLES, SMILES, AND LAUGHS 5.11c ★★★** "Ain't no sin to be glad you're alive." -Bruce Springsteen. Intricate and sustained edge pulling. Super!
   FA: Bill Ohran.

## MASS MURDER WALL

This slabby wall is littered with white calcite swirls. The climbing is characterized by smearing and suspect rock. No topo.

APPROACH: Just after the third stream crossing, bush-whack left (north) to gain a talus slope. Walk right (east) to more talus, then up 200 feet to this west facing wall. See Aerial View page 137.

1. **ALBERT FISH'S HOT DOG STAND 5.10d** Getting established over the bulge makes wieners out of most climbers. Some loose holds. The left route.
   FA: Andy Reynolds.

2. **JOHN WAYNE GACEY YOUTH EMPLOYMENT CENTER 5.10a** "Every murderer is probably somebody's old friend." -Agatha Christie. Climb up the central corner systems.
   FA: Phil and Andy Reynolds.

3. **ED GEINS CLOTHING EMPORIUM 5.10b** Several neat pocket moves are followed by loose slab climbing. A scary third clip completes the deal. The right-most route.
   FA: Phil and Andy Reynolds.

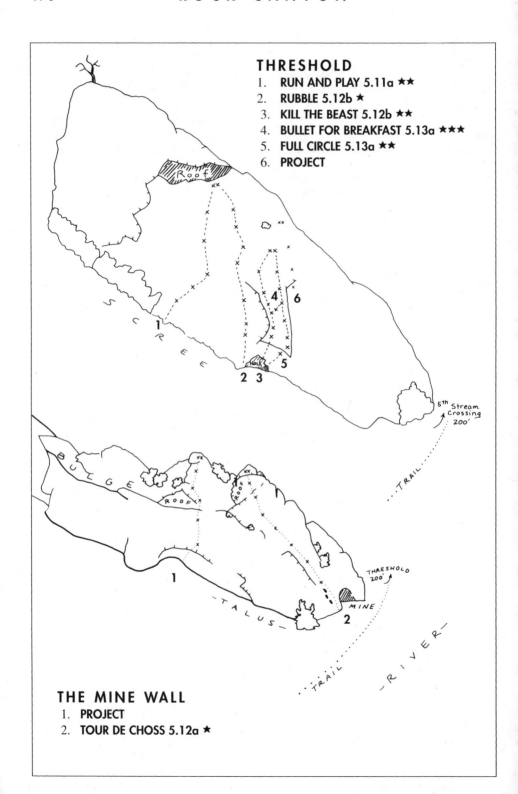

**THRESHOLD**
1. **RUN AND PLAY 5.11a ★★**
2. **RUBBLE 5.12b ★**
3. **KILL THE BEAST 5.12b ★★**
4. **BULLET FOR BREAKFAST 5.13a ★★★**
5. **FULL CIRCLE 5.13a ★★**
6. **PROJECT**

**THE MINE WALL**
1. **PROJECT**
2. **TOUR DE CHOSS 5.12a ★**

## THE MINE WALL

A quiet wall with a mine entrance at its base. The one route on the southwest face makes the most of what there is to offer. Shattered rock abounds, but **Tour De Choss** links up the solid rock, and the end result is a fine, pumpy route.

APPROACH: Approach from a small trail that stays on the left (north) side of the stream between the fourth and fifth stream crossings. The trail passes right by the obvious mine, which is located half way between the two stream crossings.See Aerial View page 137.

1. **PROJECT**

2. **TOUR DE CHOSS 5.12a** ★ Don't believe the name--only one section has loose footholds. A three stage tour across the wall that will leave you breathless. Stay low at the second bolt, persevere on the strenuous layaways in the mid section, and enjoy the cool pockets near the top.
   FA: Tim Hannig.

## THRESHOLD

**The Threshold** is a radically steep wall with numerous angular holds. The rock faces west and is a perfect summer morning wall. The limestone here resembles quartzite and favors power, strong fingers and an appetite for fun.

APPROACH: Approach from a small trail that stays on the left (north) side of the stream between the fourth and fifth stream crossings. Follow the trail up canyon 200 feet past **The Mine Wall**. or from the fifth stream crossing, walk down canyon 200 feet on the trail and schazam! Walk up the talus to reach these awesome routes. See Aerial View page 137.

1. **RUN AND PLAY 5.11a** ★★ Several balancy moves are followed by fun jug hauling. Good grips and steep stone.
   FA: Bill Ohran.

2. **RUBBLE 5.12b** ★ It's hard, but not as hard as **Chicago Overhang**. A bouldery start to good climbing, marred only by bolt placements that are a foot too high.
   FA: Tim Hannig.

3. **KILL THE BEAST 5.12b** ★★ "If it bleeds we can kill it." -Arnold Schwarzenegger. A roof problem that just won't die.
   FA: Bill Ohran.

4. **BULLET FOR BREAKFAST 5.13a** ★★★ If you can pull a door jam edge down to your kneecaps, you'll devour this test piece. Bite the bullet and cut out right on fingery holds and bad feet.
   FA: Jeff Pedersen.

5. **FULL CIRCLE 5.13a** ★★ Slopey holds, sidepulls, weirdness--all the makings of a first class route. Jeff started climbing in Rock Canyon years ago, and this route marks his return.
   FA: Jeff Pedersen.

6. **PROJECT**

Boone Speed leading **Burning [5.13b], Hell Cave,** American Fork Canyon

# HOBBLE CREEK CANYON

Hobble Creek is a quiet canyon east of Springville. Hidden within its steep, oak-covered walls are a golf course, numerous picnic sites, a lush canyon bottom with a winding river - and one developed limestone crag. Although there are only three routes here, much potential exists. The rock is sound, with edges rather then pockets forming most of the weaknesses. With southern exposure and little shade from the surrounding trees, the **Hobble Creek Cliff** is a pleasant oven in early spring and late fall. In the summer, however, the approach alone is near fatal. The climbs here are steep, long and continuous. The pleasant view, solitude and interesting climbing make Hobble Creek a good choice for climbers looking for something different. THE BOLTS COUNTS ON THESE ROUTES ARE ESTIMATES ONLY.

To reach Hobble Creek, turn off I-15 at exit 263 and follow Highway 77 east into the town of Springville. Continue through Springville on Highway 77(now 400 South) to the intersection of 400 South and 1300 East, where the road to Hobble Creek curves right. Continue along Canyon Road to a Y intersection, where the left fork leads into Hobble Creek Canyon. After the golf course, the canyon forks. Take the right fork and follow it 2.8 miles to a small pullout on the right side of the road. The limestone cliff can be seen on the north side of the road, distinguished by its impressive-looking roofs. A steep walk up the slope below the wall takes about 15 minutes, and if a careful path is chosen, it is almost brush-free.

All three routes are located on a free-standing pillar near the center of the wall. There are no topos of these climbs.

1. **HIGH NOON 5.11d ★** A long route that weaves up the south face of the pillar. A bouldery start begins near the left side of the south face and then climbs directly up the center of the wall. About 15 bolts.
   FA: Chris Laycock.

2. **I SHOT THE SHERIFF (WITH A BOSCH) 5.11d ★** Another bouldery start leads to more reasonable climbing, with the crux higher on the route. This sporty line climbs the east face, following the bolt line just right of the arête. About 10 bolts.
   FA: Boone Speed and Jeff Pedersen.

3. **HANGDOG JURY 5.12b ★** Step left off the boulder and climb the right-leaning bolt line up the center of the east face. A very difficult sequence with technical and balancy moves marks the crux, however everything about this route seems hard. About 10 bolts.
   FA: Boone Speed and Jeff Pedersen.

# INDEX OF
# ROUTES BY RATING

## 5.10

- [ ] A Rose is a Rose ★ 120
- [ ] Black Rose ★ 120
- [ ] Edge of Knight ★★★ 118
- [ ] Electric Landlady 127
- [ ] Left Unknown 163
- [ ] Meat ByProduct ★ 125
- [ ] Motherload 91
- [ ] Return of the Prince 93
- [ ] Right Unknown 163
- [ ] Serpentine 28
- [ ] Teenagers in Heat ★ 95
- [ ] Winds of Fire 86

## 5.10a

- [ ] Awakening ★ 91
- [ ] Banana Dream 111
- [ ] Barnacle 46
- [ ] Beginning, The ★★ 169
- [ ] Black Hole ★ 95
- [ ] Bosko's Mystery Pants ★ 143
- [ ] Caress of Steel ★★★ 65
- [ ] Domestic Tension ★ 45
- [ ] Dr. Teeth 139
- [ ] John Wayne Gacey
  Youth Employment Center 169
- [ ] Les is More ★ 97
- [ ] Motu ★ 27
- [ ] Necromancer ★ 93
- [ ] Pink Canoe ★ 120
- [ ] Platinum Blonde ★ 86
- [ ] Punch the Clock
  (aka "Vixen Blonde") ★ 85
- [ ] Room with a View 61
- [ ] Suicidal Yet Depraved ★ 141
- [ ] Twist and Shout ★★ 91
- [ ] Two-Nut Muffin 127
- [ ] Vengeance ★ 139
- [ ] White Line ★ 157

## 5.10b

- [ ] Bait for the Sky ★ 17
- [ ] Blood on the Rocks 47
- [ ] Bloody Fingers ★★ 169
- [ ] Bosko Loves Barbed Wire ★★ 141
- [ ] Cannabis Crack ★ 61
- [ ] Ed Geins Clothing Emporium 169
- [ ] Harder-Faster 93
- [ ] Jug for Joy ★★ 91
- [ ] Leapin' Lizards ★★ 43
- [ ] Patty Baby ★ 103
- [ ] Sex Farm ★ 149
- [ ] Steel Graffia ★ 91
- [ ] Zoo, The ★ 147

## 5.10b/c

- [ ] Shortness 105

## 5.10c

- [ ] Cambrian Grey ★★★ 141
- [ ] Crack 157
- [ ] Denied ★ 91
- [ ] Hidden, The ★★ 163
- [ ] Lacy Doggie Panties ★ 141
- [ ] Persona Non Grata ★ 43
- [ ] Sundance ★ 30

## 5.10c/d

- [ ] Metal ★★ 163

## 5.10d

- ☐ Afterglow ★ 29
- ☐ Albert Fish's Hot Dog Stand 169
- ☐ Bosko is a Cruel Master ★★ 143
- ☐ Boskoizer ★ 143
- ☐ Captured for Rapture ★★ 118
- ☐ Crescendo ★★ 29
- ☐ Desperate Land ★ 141
- ☐ Drop Anchor ★ 27
- ☐ Erase Your Face ★★ 127
- ☐ Green Monster Aid Crack ★★★ 127
- ☐ Honey, the Virgin Seductress ★ 143
- ☐ Impossible Dream ★★ 117
- ☐ Inside Information ★★ 91
- ☐ Mausoleum 142
- ☐ Monkey Meet ★★★ 91
- ☐ Mr. Numbers ★ 129
- ☐ Roaches on a Face ★★ 118
- ☐ Seacliff ★ 27
- ☐ Smell the Glove ★★ 149
- ☐ Steel Monkey ★★ 65
- ☐ Sweetness 105
- ☐ Topaz 28
- ☐ Vomit ★ 158
- ☐ Wilber, Honey's Naughty Pussy ★★ 143

## 5.10d/.11a

- ☐ Hot Sun ★ 25

## 5.11

- ☐ Inner Limits ★★ 118
- ☐ Legos ★ 127
- ☐ Necrophilia 17
- ☐ Pure Thoughts ★★ 127
- ☐ Technical Difficulties 149

## 5.11a

- ☐ Bad Beta ★ 58
- ☐ Billy Goat's Gruff 45
- ☐ Body Bag ★★ 91
- ☐ Chernobyl 35
- ☐ Chicago's East Side ★ 129
- ☐ Contusion Dweller ★ 105
- ☐ Cool World ★★ 167
- ☐ Cranial Bypass ★ 47
- ☐ Deep End ★★ 95
- ☐ Dreamin' of Reamin' ★ 141
- ☐ Drill for the Redeemer, The ★ 17
- ☐ Excessive Bail ★★ 147
- ☐ Fishwife ★ 152
- ☐ Necrobeastiality ★★ 141
- ☐ Obsessive Tendencies 113
- ☐ Pocket Change ★ 97
- ☐ Raid ★ 141
- ☐ Remote Control ★ 97
- ☐ Riptide ★ 65
- ☐ Run and Play ★★ 171
- ☐ Running Woman ★ 97
- ☐ Seek and Enjoy 27
- ☐ Small Change ★ 74
- ☐ Squid Orgy ★ 141
- ☐ Tour De Choss ★ 171
- ☐ Wasp, The 115
- ☐ Zulu ★ 67

## 5.11a/b

- ☐ Everest 101 ★ 113
- ☐ Naive Guitar ★ 25
- ☐ Piece of Meat ★★ 125
- ☐ Shunned Freedom ★ 23

## 5.11b

- [ ] 39 ★★ 97
- [ ] Atheist, The ★★ 97
- [ ] Autonomy ★ 59
- [ ] Baghdad ★★ 97
- [ ] Bitch School ★★ 149
- [ ] Blue Moon ★ 21
- [ ] Blurred Vision ★ 97
- [ ] Brave Words ★★ 169
- [ ] Bulge, The ★ 131
- [ ] Choss Fighter 19
- [ ] Cosmological Retreat ★ 65
- [ ] Dead on Arrival ★ 91
- [ ] Distorted and Thin ★ 101
- [ ] Electric Company ★★ 61
- [ ] Feral Neurons ★ 67
- [ ] Firewoman ★★ 45
- [ ] Got Caught Stealing ★ 161
- [ ] Green Hornet , The★ 115
- [ ] Inferior ★★ 152
- [ ] Juggernaut ★★★ 87
- [ ] Killer Wasp 115
- [ ] Mutilation ★★ 152
- [ ] Narcolepsy ★ 93
- [ ] On Wings of Beagles ★ 57
- [ ] Pieces of Iraq ★ 25
- [ ] Primal Magic 85
- [ ] Redneck Genocide ★★ 141
- [ ] Romeo's Bleeding ★ 51
- [ ] Rush Hour ★ 97
- [ ] Sesame Street ★ 61
- [ ] Shallow Beginning ★★ 95
- [ ] Simple Simon ★★ 113
- [ ] Suicide Blonde ★★ 85
- [ ] Sun King ★ 45
- [ ] Wasatch Pickles ★★ 67
- [ ] We're Not in Kansas Anymore ★ 161

## 5.11b/c

- [ ] Bikini Wax ★ 29
- [ ] Edge of Chaos, The ★ 89
- [ ] Eight to Eleven ★ 86
- [ ] High, Hard One, The ★ 113
- [ ] Lightning Bolt ★ 147
- [ ] Sans Nom ★ 89
- [ ] Tracks ★★ 157
- [ ] Welcome to the Crux ★★ 169

## 5.11c

- [ ] Atrocious ★ 158
- [ ] Big Bottoms ★★ 149
- [ ] Cranial Impact ★★ 47
- [ ] Deadman's Party ★ 145
- [ ] Distraction ★ 37
- [ ] Fang 73
- [ ] Furious ★ 158
- [ ] Greener Over There 71
- [ ] Grins, Giggles, Smiles, and Laughs ★★★ 169
- [ ] Gripcom 71
- [ ] Hitcher ★ 35
- [ ] License to Thrill ★★★ 65
- [ ] Litmus Test ★★ 95
- [ ] Matilda ★ 45
- [ ] Nowhere to Go 97
- [ ] Reel Value ★ 71
- [ ] Slimabeing ★ 81
- [ ] Snakejuice ★ 165
- [ ] Spring Madness ★★ 101
- [ ] Stilletto ★★ 151
- [ ] Superintendent's Limp Dicks ★ 57
- [ ] Weaned on a Pickle ★ 21
- [ ] Yuji Feet ★ 120

## 5.11c/d

- [ ] Anarchist, The ★ 75
- [ ] Choss Fire ★ 19
- [ ] Premise, The ★ 81
- [ ] Razor Clam ★★ 28
- [ ] Stay on the Porch ★ 37

## 5.11d

- [ ] Avalanche ★ 105
- [ ] Bad Bananas 111
- [ ] BFE ★★★ 145
- [ ] Cyberlag ★★ 85
- [ ] Dazed and Refused ★ 123
- [ ] Desperate But Not Serious ★ 59
- [ ] Division ★★★ 97
- [ ] Ectopic Distress 57
- [ ] Erection or Ejection ★★ 74
- [ ] Evolution or Regression? 23
- [ ] Facelift ★★ 101
- [ ] High Noon ★ 173
- [ ] I Shot the Sheriff (With a Bosch) ★ 173
- [ ] Invitation to the Blues ★★ 74
- [ ] Learning to Fly ★★★ 165
- [ ] Liposuction ★ 101
- [ ] Little Big Wall ★ 65
- [ ] Memorial Park 142
- [ ] Music for Chameleons ★★ 75
- [ ] Neosymian Thugs ★ 119
- [ ] Price is Right, The ★ 37
- [ ] RDA ★ 19
- [ ] Reaching for Razors ★★ 51
- [ ] Screaming Lobsters ★ 28
- [ ] Shark Club ★ 95
- [ ] She Sells Sanctuary ★★ 17
- [ ] Spank ★ 158
- [ ] Spatial Unrest ★ 57
- [ ] Spawning ★★ 45
- [ ] Suspect ★★ 57
- [ ] Swing Shift 111
- [ ] Total Recall ★★ 97
- [ ] Virtual Reality ★ 89

## 5.11d/.12a

- [ ] Teeanova ★★★ 85

## 5.12

- [ ] Apetizer ★★★ 73
- [ ] Bad Dreams 103
- [ ] Cinnamon Bay ★★ 28
- [ ] Margarita ★★★ 28
- [ ] Sea Tomato ★★ 28
- [ ] Spam ★★ 125

## 5.12a

- [ ] Argument, The ★ 81
- [ ] Blanket Party ★ 151
- [ ] Blight, The ★ 51
- [ ] C'est Cool ★★ 147
- [ ] Club ★ 73
- [ ] Death of a Sailsman ★★ 75
- [ ] Direct Start ★★ 101
- [ ] Dogma ★ 47
- [ ] Empiricist ★ 47
- [ ] Fat Hippos ★ 120
- [ ] Field of Screams ★★ 61
- [ ] Gateway ★★ 55
- [ ] Half Acre ★ 55
- [ ] Hate ★ 156
- [ ] Jitterbug Boy ★★ 51
- [ ] Liquid Oxygen ★★★ 95
- [ ] Mandela ★★ 65
- [ ] Meadow Muffin ★★★ 127
- [ ] Mission Control ★ 61
- [ ] Mother of Invention ★★ 133
- [ ] Naked Nebula ★★ 89
- [ ] One, The ★ 73
- [ ] Organ Grinder ★ 21
- [ ] Orogeny ★★★ 38
- [ ] Osmosis ★ 43
- [ ] Pocket Debris ★★★ 99
- [ ] Route 66 ★★ 65
- [ ] Shinobi ★★ 35
- [ ] Sister Ray ★ 19
- [ ] Slacker ★★★ 165
- [ ] Smash the Poser ★ 113
- [ ] Spoons and Needles ★★ 157
- [ ] Step Right Up ★★★ 45
- [ ] Stretchmarks ★ 19
- [ ] Struggling Man ★★ 97
- [ ] Touch of Grey ★★ 43
- [ ] Wasatch Reality ★ 52
- [ ] Wasted and Wounded ★ 46
- [ ] Whining, The ★ 74
- [ ] Wooden Kimono 142

## 5.12a/.12b/c

- [ ] American Flyers ★★  75
- [ ] Gridlock ★★  75

## 5.12a/b

- [ ] Active Transport ★  43
- [ ] All Men are Mortal ★★  81
- [ ] Ambush ★★  74
- [ ] Blimp Factor ★  99
- [ ] Isotoner Moaner ★★★  97
- [ ] Kin-A ★★  165
- [ ] Lion Fish ★  28
- [ ] Neural Processor ★★  99
- [ ] Nuclear Criminal ★  35
- [ ] Pig Pen ★★  103
- [ ] Punch the Clock Roof ★  86
- [ ] Return to Sender ★  105
- [ ] Too Young to be Human ★★★  81
- [ ] Unknown Pleasures ★★  43
- [ ] Wilderness ★  62

## 5.12b

- [ ] Bamboo ★★★  27
- [ ] Beehive ★★  85
- [ ] Beeline ★★★  75
- [ ] Book of Condolences ★★★  19
- [ ] Closer ★  43
- [ ] Dark Rum ★★  27
- [ ] Drain ★★  152
- [ ] Dreadlocks ★★  85
- [ ] F.Away ★★  151
- [ ] Ferocious ★★  158
- [ ] Gorillas in the Snow ★★  73
- [ ] Hangdog Jury ★  173
- [ ] Hanky Head ★  29
- [ ] Helix ★★★  37
- [ ] Kill the Beast ★★  171
- [ ] Ladies First (Variation) ★  152
- [ ] Let's Pretend ★  45
- [ ] Maritime ★★  29
- [ ] Merciless Onslaught ★★  61
- [ ] Rubble ★  171
- [ ] Secret Weapon ★  97
- [ ] Sharkfighter ★★  43
- [ ] Spinoza ★  45
- [ ] Substance ★★  43
- [ ] To Kill a Chalkingbird ★  45
- [ ] Tulsa ★  37
- [ ] White Trash ★  156
- [ ] Woodstock ★  103
- [ ] Xcess ★★  19

## 5.12b/.12c/d

- [ ] To Hell on a Rocket ★★  75

## 5.12b/c

- [ ] Air Blast ★  105
- [ ] Algorithm ★★★  99
- [ ] Black Heart ★  99
- [ ] Isolation ★★  62
- [ ] Juggernaut Roof ★★★  85
- [ ] One That Got Away, The ★★  74
- [ ] Runaway Train ★  73
- [ ] Slip Slopin' Away ★★  19

## 5.12b/c

- [ ] Black Magic ★★  37

## 5.12c

- Bermuda Shorts ★★ 29
- Curbjob ★★ 152
- Drogen ★★ 151
- Dwarf Toss ★★ 74
- Easter Island ★ 27
- Flight Fright ★ 65
- Hideaway ★ 27
- I'll Take Black ★ 55
- Lurch ★ 152
- Megadose ★★ 19
- Problem Child ★★ 37
- True Lies ★★ 37

## 5.12c/d

- Abyss, The ★★ 95
- Close Your Eyes and Fantasize ★★ 119
- Left for Dead ★★ 99
- Siberia ★ 62
- Syllogism ★★★ 81

## 5.12d

- Bats Out of Hell ★ 52
- Bon Voyage ★ 27
- Dead Devil ★★ 152
- Drifting 28
- Eating the Gun ★★ 74
- Forty Something ★★ 81
- Green Violetear ★★★ 28
- Guillotine ★★ 51
- Knuckle Up ★★★ 89
- Nihilist, The ★★ 47
- Reanimator ★★ 51
- Shadowplay ★★ 43
- Silencer ★ 19
- Slumlord ★★ 152
- Something Wild ★★ 61

## 5.12d/.13a

- El Diablo ★★ 55
- Melting ★★★ 52
- This Must be the Pickle ★★ 74

## 5.13

- Minimalist 19

## 5.13a

- Alcyone ★★★ 28
- Atmosphere ★★★ 74
- Blue Typhoon ★★★ 28
- Bullet for Breakfast ★★★ 171
- Full Circle ★★ 171
- Gutterboy ★★ 152
- Malvado ★★ 55
- Monkey Brains ★★★ 73
- No Quarters ★ 21
- Oz ★ 52
- Teardrop ★★ 61
- Tropical Depression ★★ 27
- Underdog ★★★ 61
- Undertow ★ 28
- X ★★★ 19
- Xtension ★★ 19

## 5.13a/b

- Hell ★★★ 51
- Jug Abuse ★★ 61

## 5.13b

- [ ] Burning ★★★ 52
- [ ] Citrus ★★★ 28
- [ ] Decades ★★ 45
- [ ] Inferno ★★ 55
- [ ] Junkie Bitch ★★ 151
- [ ] Junkie Pride ★★★ 151
- [ ] Mr. Concrete ★★ 152
- [ ] Redrum ★★★ 74
- [ ] Snaked from New York ★ 81
- [ ] White Noise ★★ 55
- [ ] Wizards ★★★ 52

## 5.13b/c

- [ ] Invisible Man ★★★ 74
- [ ] Simian ★★ 37
- [ ] Valhalla ★★★ 152

## 5.13c

- [ ] Blue Mask ★★★ 74
- [ ] Fryeing ★★★ 52
- [ ] High Water ★★ 51
- [ ] Linus ★★ 52
- [ ] Shining, The ★★★ 74
- [ ] Side Show Bob's ★★ 52
- [ ] Soul Fission ★★ 55

## 5.13c/d

- [ ] Watch Your Face ★★ 151

## 5.13d

- [ ] Body Count ★★★ 55
- [ ] Brimstone (Variation) ★★ 51
- [ ] Hey Whitey ★★★ 151
- [ ] Loveboat ★ 79
- [ ] Power Junkie ★★★ 55
- [ ] Satanism and Sports ★★ 55

## 5.13d/.14a

- [ ] Blow of Death
  (aka Dead Souls) ★★★ 55
- [ ] Cannibals ★★★ 52
- [ ] Cop Killer ★★ 55
- [ ] I Scream 52

## 5.14a

- [ ] Higher Water (Variation) ★★ 51

# INDEX BY ROUTE NAME

# Point.
# Click.
# Send.

**Climbing.com**

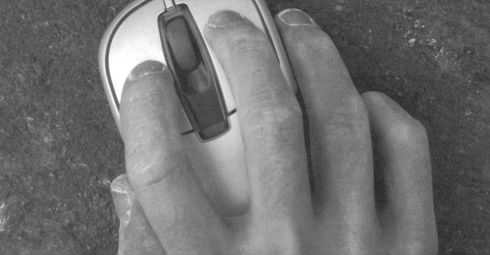

# Access: It's everybody's concern

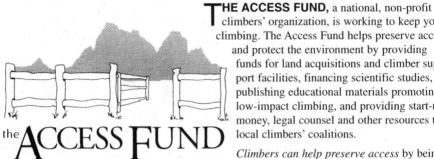

**the ACCESS FUND**

**T**HE **ACCESS FUND,** a national, non-profit climbers' organization, is working to keep you climbing. The Access Fund helps preserve access and protect the environment by providing funds for land acquisitions and climber support facilities, financing scientific studies, publishing educational materials promoting low-impact climbing, and providing start-up money, legal counsel and other resources to local climbers' coalitions.

*Climbers can help preserve access* by being responsible users of climbing areas. Here are some practical ways to support climbing:

- **COMMIT YOURSELF TO "ZERO IMPACT."** Pick up litter around campgrounds and the crags. Let your actions inspire others.

- **DISPOSE OF HUMAN WASTE PROPERLY.** Use toilets whenever possible. If none are available, choose a spot at least 50 meters from any water source. Dig a hole 6 inches (15 cm) deep, and bury your waste in it. *Always pack out toilet paper* in a "Zip-Lock"-type bag.

- **UTILIZE EXISTING TRAILS.** Avoid cutting switchbacks and trampling vegetation.

- **USE DISCRETION WHEN PLACING BOLTS AND OTHER "FIXED" PROTECTION.** Camouflage all anchors with rock-colored paint. Use chains for rappel stations, or leave rock-colored webbing.

- **RESPECT RESTRICTIONS THAT PROTECT NATURAL RESOURCES AND CULTURAL ARTIFACTS .** Appropriate restrictions can include prohibition of climbing around Indian rock art, pioneer inscriptions, and on certain formations during raptor nesting season. Power drills are illegal in wilderness areas. *Never chisel or sculpt holds in rock on public lands, unless it is expressly allowed* – no other practice so seriously threatens our sport.

- **PARK IN DESIGNATED AREAS,** not in undeveloped, vegetated areas. Carpool to the crags!

- **MAINTAIN A LOW PROFILE.** Other people have the same right to undisturbed enjoyment of natural areas as do you.

- **RESPECT PRIVATE PROPERTY.** Don't trespass in order to climb.

- **JOIN OR FORM A GROUP TO DEAL WITH ACCESS ISSUES IN YOUR AREA.** Consider clean-ups, trail building or maintenance, or other "goodwill" projects.

- **JOIN THE ACCESS FUND.** To become a member, *simply make a donation (tax-deductable) of any amount.* Only by working together can we preserve the diverse American climbing experience.

**The Access Fund. Preserving America's diverse climbing resources.**
The Access Fund • P.O. Box 17010 • Boulder, CO 80308